SECRET KEEPER
Devotional

A 35-Day Experience with
The **Delicate Power** of **Modesty**

DANNAH GRESH

MOODY PUBLISHERS
CHICAGO

Unless otherwise indicated, Scripture quotations are from the *Holy Bible, New International Version®*. NIV®. Copyright © 1973, 1978, 1984 by International Bible Society. Used by permission of Zondervan Publishing House. All rights reserved.

Scripture quotations marked NASB are taken from the *New American Standard Bible®*, copyright © 1960, 1962, 1968, 1971, 1972, 1973, 1975, 1977, 1995 by The Lockman Foundation. Used by permission. (www. Lockman.org)

Scripture quotations marked MESSAGE are from *The Message*, copyright © by Eugene H. Peterson 1993, 1994, 1995, 1996, 2000, 2001, 2002, 2003. Used by permission of NavPress Publishing Group. All rights reserved.

ISBN: 978-0-8024-0253-0
Printed by Versa Press in East Peoria, IL – October 2011

Library of Congress Cataloging-in-Publication Data
Gresh, Dannah.
    Secret keeper devotional : a 35-day experience with the delicate power of modesty / Dannah Gresh.
        p. cm.
    Includes bibliographical references (p. 154).
    ISBN 978-0-8024-0253-0
    1. Young women--Religious life--Textbooks. 2. Young women--Conduct of life--Textbooks. 3. Teenage girls--Conduct of life--Textbooks.
    4. Modesty--Religious aspects--Christianity--Textbooks. 5. Clothing and dress--Religious aspects--Christianity--Textbooks. I. Title.
    BV4551.3.G755 2011
    248.8'33--dc23
                                2011018573

Cover Design: LeVan Fisher Design
Cover Image: © PhotoAlto/Sigrid Olsson/Getty Images
Interior Design: Julia Ryan | www.DesignByJulia.com
Interior Photos & Images: Teens: Steve Tressler (Vista Photography)

We hope you enjoy this book from Moody Publishers. Our goal is to provide high-quality, thought-provoking books and products that connect truth to your real needs and challenges. For more information on other books and products written and produced from a biblical perspective, go to www.moodypublishers.com or write to:

Moody Publishers
820 N. LaSalle Boulevard
Chicago, IL 60610

3 5 7 9 10 8 6 4 2

Printed in the United States of America

It is written: "No eye has seen,

no ear has heard, no mind has conceived

what God has prepared for those who love him" —

but God has revealed it to us by his Spirit.

The Spirit searches all things,

even the deep things of God.

1 Corinthians 2:9–10

THE SPIRIT

CONTENTS

The Power } An Invitation to Go Deep!

EVERY NERVE IN MY BODY WAS FILLED WITH THRILLING TINGLES OF EXCITEMENT. My husband, Bob, and I were in the Bahamas, and we were about to take our very first dive. Yes, as in SCUBA dive!

After a quick twenty-minute instruction session in a calm, cool swimming pool, I was loading my equipment and heading out to view the underwater wonders of the ocean. I couldn't wait.

As our little boat chugged out from the dock, the thrill became uncontainable. I closed my eyes and allowed the sun to warm my face as I entered into a quiet but enthusiastic conversation with the God of the universe.

"Lord, You know I'll be ministering to a large group in Atlanta next weekend," I prayed silently. "It would be so cool if You'd give me a powerful word picture during this dive—something to teach them in a compelling way. Could You please show me Your wonder?" I was just certain that God was going to show up in a big way during this dive.

❤ Wham!

The boat was hit with the first of what would be many nasty waves. We rocked back and forth as our captain navigated us purposefully toward our dive site. Every now and then another huge wave would crash over the back of the boat during our continuous rocking through three-foot waves. After a few minutes, I noticed Bob wasn't doing too well. He tends to get seasick, and these were the worst waves we'd ridden in some time.

"You okay?" I asked.

"I will be just as soon as I get under these waves," he said.

We both knew that needed to happen soon.

We got to the dive site.

"Hmmmm . . . this wasn't what I'd pictured," I thought looking around. I imagined being out on a calm ocean where I'd be able to comfortably get used to my equipment before I took the plunge. That plan wasn't looking so good. I pulled my equipment on and stood at the edge of the boat. I was scared silly!

Bob jumped in with the instructor.

I just stood there.

Frozen.

The waves beat against my legs, hitting as high as my thighs as I clung to the boat's shiny, metal stair rail.

The instructor kept calling to me. Bob kept giving me the diver's sign for "Everything's okay!" They waited and encouraged me.

For a long time.

I just stood there.

Finally, I closed my eyes and jumped. My mouth gauge went flailing through the air behind me. Once I was in, I realized what a bad idea it was not to have my mouth gauge in. I reached for it.

Wham!

A wave knocked it out of my hands.
I tried again.

Wham!

Where was that instructor?

WHAM!

Wham!

I couldn't find it.

Wham!

Each wave engulfed me in nasty, salty water.

Wham!

"I've got to get out!" I heard Bob yelling frantically, sending a new and more powerful wave of fear through me.

Wham!

Another wave!

I saw Bob clamoring as he used the boat's rope to pull himself in. That was all the encouragement I needed. I was headin' back in.

I began to race toward him, finding the rope myself. As we neared the boat, I wrapped my legs and arms around Bob, who'd found the metal ladder.

"Let go of your husband," I heard the instructor shouting over the noise of the water. I didn't want to let go. My husband was my confidence! I knew he would not let me get swept away in these waves.

I would not let go.

"Let go if you want to get in," he demanded as he pried me off of Bob's body.

Wham!

I was out in the water again.

Bob was almost on deck.

What on earth?

Wham!

As I faced yet another horrendous wave, I could see Bob standing on the edge of the boat.

He was barfing! The source of my security was barfing on the boat!

I swam back to the ladder, and a crew member pulled me up. I was beyond bummed. So much for the wonders of the ocean!

"Didn't we have a plan, God?" I asked a few minutes later as we rested in the boat. "Weren't You going to show me an amazing and powerful word picture to teach Your truth?"

As clear as if it had been Bob speaking next to me, I heard God's voice speak inside of me: *I did.*

I was puzzled. I couldn't for the life of me see what He meant.

There was one other diver on our trip that day. She was experienced, and the instructor took her under after he got us back into the boat. After about twenty minutes, they came up, and before she was even in the boat she began to speak of the wonder.

"We caught a blowfish and made it blow up." She giggled. "There were blue and yellow . . ." On and on she went, unable to contain the wonder.

That was it. I saw it!

This was, in fact, an amazing picture of truth from my precious God. Too many believers today are discouraged in their faith because they're stuck on the surface. They're unwilling to devote themselves to the difficult task of "going deep." And they cannot understand why they don't see God's wonders.

The next day, gluttons for punishment, Bob and I hired Captain Phil. He promised us a smooth and successful snorkeling experience. As horrible as our experience had been the day before, we were passionate about seeing what was under that surface! We were willing to embarrass ourselves once again for another try.

Five others were on this trip. One guy, I was certain, was a member of the Mafia. Tough. Unemployed. Pockets filled with hundred-dollar bills. Spoke of working for "the family" once. You do the math. I say this only because, if there's ever peer pressure to be cool, I guess it's when the Mafia is around.

A few minutes later I was under the surface.

WOW!

Enthusiasm burst out from my being. The beauty, the purple tapestries of coral amazed me. They were like delicate paintings waving in the ocean. Entire schools of fish swam around me. My eyes couldn't take it all in.

A huge purple and green and yellow fish swam by—a parrot fish. I sprang up from the surface.

"Look! Look!" I shouted to the others, including the Mafia guy, knowing that I looked very, very uncool. Extreme enthusiasm will do that to you. Coolness factor tanks!

"You've got to see this," I cried as I slipped back under the surface again to see a long, slender brown fish that looked like an eel. It was a cigar fish.

"Did you see that?" I shouted, making a fool of myself once again.

I was the last one out of the water.

{ **IT'S WORTH IT TO GO AGAINST THE CURRENT OF TODAY'S BUSYNESS AND SCREEN-SATURATED CULTURE.**

Do you ever feel that your walk of faith lacks power? Do you ever read passages about God's miraculous power and wonder why you've never seen much of that? Do you tire of hearing or even seeing others experience God, only to find that your own experience of Him isn't nearly as wondrous? Do you ever look around your congregation and wish there were someone to rescue you but you only see others clamoring for God's rescue just like you? Do you hear your youth leaders trying to teach you what they believe is a powerful truth only to find it means nothing to you personally? Do you want to see His wonders? Do you want God's truth to excite you to the inner core? Then you've got to go deep!

First Corinthians 2:9–10 reads, "It is written: 'No eye has seen, no ear has heard, no mind has conceived what God has prepared for those who love him'—but God has revealed it to us by his Spirit. The Spirit searches all things, even the deep things of God."

GO DEEP

You cannot imagine the mind-blowing things God has for you under the surface. But God promises that when we meet His Spirit in a powerful way, we will have even the deep things of God revealed to us.

You won't find the amazing treasures of God up on the surface. They can't be found in superficial conversations at church or just attending youth group. You've got to go deep. Go deep into His Word when you're alone. Talk about the secret things of God with friends at church. Dive into the truth your pastor presents. It's not easy to go deep. It takes time. You have to go against the current of today's busyness and screen-saturated culture. You'll find yourself discouraged sometimes, but I do believe you and I, together, can go deep in the next thirty days.

Although thousands of young women have read *Secret Keeper*, far too many haven't really "gotten it." They walk up to me expressing excitement about the message of beauty and modesty, but, since these messages are ones that lead to visible results, I can see that they haven't gotten the message of the book.

Some get it for a few weeks or even months, but then their youth pastor reports they're wearing seductive clothes once again, always in the name of fashion. They mean to dress modestly, but they're so influenced by culture that the change doesn't stick.

These girls are stuck on the surface. Because of that, they don't understand the beauty and power with which they've been crafted by the God of the universe.

I want to take you more deeply into truth. Will you dive below the surface with me?

You can learn from these devotions on your own, or you can do them with a group, in which case you'll have weekly meetings with some fun activities. (The group leader, who might be you, will find these activities in the appendix at the back of the book.) Either way, you'll be doing five days of devotions each week to coincide with each chapter of *Secret Keeper*. You don't really need to read *Secret Keeper* the week you read the devotions, but you can, and I encourage you to. It'll just plant more great stuff in your head. You'll find that the devotions are very loosely aligned. Watch for the little "What does SK say?" sidebar. It'll remind you to pull out the book and find the truth from that chapter that is the focus of your current devotional. The point of these devotions isn't to be repetitious; rather, the purpose is to take you a little deeper into the truth about modesty so you can really get it into your heart.

Don't skip over or skimp on any of the assignments given here. Please! You'll come up at the end having never gone deep enough to see what it's all about! Each devotional offers a Bible passage to read, some encouragement, and then a journaling assignment. You can write your journal entry in this book. Make sure you do write. You'll miss the wonder if you don't.

♥ WILL YOU "GO DEEP" WITH ME?
LET'S TAKE THE PLUNGE!

 **WHAT DOES SK SAY?** "This week's devotions are way different from the content of chapter 1 in *Secret Keeper*. God is pulling us deep because that's where His power is! But you need my little introduction from *Secret Keeper* chapter 1 to understand the power that can be found in modesty."—Dannah Gresh

DAY 1

{ "Come, all you who are thirsty, come to the waters." Isaiah 55:1

WELL, HERE YOU ARE.

How do you feel today?

Beautiful or boring?

Well-groomed or well-worn?

Are you feeling overweight? Or tanned and toned?

Are your friendships building you up and giving you courage? Or have they left you raw and lonely?

Is your heart in a good place and filled with strength, or does your spirit feel wilted? All too often, I find that girls and women who dress immodestly are simply hiding a wilted spirit.

I experienced a really painful time a few years ago. During that time, I dressed to the "nines," as they say. (Where on earth did that expression come from?) I purposefully set out to tell the world I was okay, when, in fact, I was wounded. On one particularly painful day, I asked a friend who is a wonderful truth-teller, "What do you sense in me?"

"A wilted spirit," she empathized.

Tears flowed. I felt pretty wilted.

My friend prayed specifically for God to water my soul. Funny thing—He did! The next morning I just happened to read Isaiah 55, as I'd been reading through that particular book of the Bible.

"Come, all you who are thirsty, come to the waters. . . . As the rain and the snow come down from heaven, and do not return to it without watering the earth and making it bud and flourish, so that it yields seed for the sower and bread for the eater, so is my word that goes out from my mouth: It will not return to me empty, but will accomplish what I desire and achieve the purpose for which I sent it. You will go out in joy and be led forth in peace" (verses 1, 10–12).

Are you feeling wilted? At the end of your rope? GO DEEP! Get into His Word. He promises that He can water your wilted spirit! He promises that His Word will accomplish something fantastic. Dare to go deep. And, I promise, you'll come out in joy!

❤ **IN YOUR JOURNAL TODAY** . . . Rewrite your favorite part of Isaiah 55 as a prayer. For example, "Oh Lord, I am thirsty and I come to You. Your Word is like water to me . . . " Today, just pour out prayer!

DARE
TO GO
DEEP

{ As the deer pants for streams of water, so my soul pants for you, O God. Psalm 42:1

DO YOU KNOW THAT IT'S OKAY TO HAVE A WILTED SPIRIT? That it's okay to be thirsty? What's not okay is trying to quench that thirst with clothes, relationships, spending flings, and entertainment that's ungodly. But, if you're like me, you've had a brownie or two when you feel bad about yourself. Sadly, it never makes me feel much better; it only adds a little weight.

On June 12, 2003, I lay outside my little cabin at a camp in northern California, reading God's Word. Though it was summer, the mountain above me was still capped in snow. What a sight! The snow was melting at a rapid pace, causing a tremendous flow of raging, cold, crystal-clear water to rush into the little creek beside me.

I just happened to read Psalm 42 that morning, which reads, "As the deer pants for streams of water, so my soul pants for you, O God." I laid my head down to pray about that. *Just how thirsty do I have to get, God, for You to really quench me?*

Suddenly I wondered to myself if any deer ever wandered into this well-populated campground for the quenching power of this little creek. I opened my eyes, and there, ten feet in front of me, was a young deer, looking frightened and frail but purposefully stepping toward the creek. Wow! Was I blown away! It was as if God were saying, Be this thirsty, Dannah! Dare to go to places you've not been, to wander into unfamiliar territory, to be seen by those you'd rather not have see you thirst for Me. That's how thirsty!

I'm praying you'll experience this kind of a moment with God during our thirty-day plunge. I hope you'll see His wonder as He brings you a deer—or a friend with godly advice or a new moment of clarity from His Word.

Oh, but you have to be thirsty—thirsty enough to not believe the lies this world tells you about how you should look, talk, and act, thirsty enough to step away from the crowd into a new place. Are you that thirsty?

{
♥ **IN YOUR JOURNAL TODAY** . . . Today in your journal I want you to confess to God what things you've tried to use to quench your thirst. What have you tried to find power in other than Him? Clothes? Guys? Popularity? Perfectionism as a student? What area do you need to turn from to walk closer to the true source of refreshing in your life?

ARE YOU THAT
THIRSTY?

{ Deep calls to deep at the sound of Your waterfalls; all Your breakers and Your waves have rolled over me. Psalm 42:7 NASB

AS YOU KNOW, MY FIRST SCUBA DIVE WASN'T A GREAT EXPERIENCE. Oh, how I wished it had been. But only one day later I had an awesome experience with snorkeling. Captain Phil took Bob and me out past the "breaker." The breaker is where the calm ocean begins to get nasty because it hits an object such as a coral reef. One side of the breaker is chaos; . . . on the other side is perfect peace. We were let out on the peaceful side and warned again and again never to get close to the breaker unless we wanted a few broken limbs and wounds as the ocean would smash us against the coral reef. If you're not careful, you can be coasting along looking at the amazing wonders of the underwater world, and you suddenly find yourself having to swim HARD for safety!

Have you ever been on the wrong side of the breaker emotionally, or spiritually? Where you feel like just yesterday you were amazed by God, and suddenly you just feel like you are too close to the edge? Or maybe you are actually OVER THE EDGE.

You're not alone. In Psalm 42, David writes about feeling like the breakers and waves had rolled over him. A closer look at the passage reveals that in Hebrew he said the "waterspouts" (not the waterfalls) called out to him. A waterspout is a large tube of clouds formed by electricity that has been trapped in fluid. It has a particular kind of circular motion at the point like a tornado; being hollow inside, it attracts vast quantities of water, which it pours down in torrents upon the earth. These spouts are frequent on the coast of Syria, and no doubt the psalmist had often seen them and the ravages waterspouts made. He felt as if he were being called into that very place.

Ever feel like that? As if you can see a twisting torrent of terror screaming your name? Maybe it's too much schoolwork, a bad relationship at home, sin you can't get away from. Today is the day to pour it out. Pour it out just like David did. Let God know how overwhelmed you feel. Tell Him how close the breakers are. Tell Him you feel "deep" calling to your deep need. But remember how David chose to end his crying. He said, "Hope in God, for I shall yet praise Him" (verse 11, NASB). Can you do that today? Choose to praise Him, even if it's hard.

As women who struggle to accept how God has created us, we often need to be truthful about how we feel. If we're not, we never really get out of the waterspout.

{ ♥ **IN YOUR JOURNAL TODAY** . . . Rewrite Psalm 42:7 and pour your heart out to God just as David did. Be sure to end with a choice to praise Him!

CHOOSE
TO PRAISE
HIM, EVEN
IF IT'S
HARD.

WEEK 1
THE POWER

DAY 4

Read Psalm 34

{ Fear the Lord, you his saints, for those who fear him lack nothing.
Psalm 34:9

THERE'S A PICTURE IN NATIONAL GEOGRAPHIC WITH A MAN'S FACE IN THE BACKGROUND THAT HORRIFIES ME.
It's not because he looks terrified or ugly, but because he looks bored. He's got his chin parked on his perched-up hand as if he can hardly stay awake during the show. What show? A lingerie show. Two beautiful women parade in front of him. One is wearing a lacy bra and bikini bottoms. The other dons a corset laced tightly to complement her satin panties.

And he's bored.

Do you see a problem here? Do you understand why I'm terrified?

If we keep selling the female body at the pace we've been selling it, soon all men will be so bored out of their gourd that there will be little left to satisfy or excite them. We will have completely relinquished our power to be alluring simply because we've been complacent about giving ourselves away cheaply in a quest for faux power.

The Journal of Advertising published a study of the effects of using overtly sexual content in mainstream consumer advertising. It reports that sexual appeal in ads does increase the interest in the product, but at the same time brand recognition was noticeably lower.[1] In other words, if the makers of Kleenex brand tissues used sexy models, they'd probably have more memorable commercials and consumers might even become consumed with tissues (the product) thinking that they might be sexier if they used tissues, but they'd be LESS likely to remember that it is Kleenex (the actual brand) tissues they're supposed to be buying.

This makes me wonder: If you follow the trend of dressing sexy, acting sexy, talking sexy, won't you also be creating a higher level of interest in the sexual appeal of women in general (the product) while at the same time making yourself (the particular brand) more generic and uninteresting?

I think a lot of women today dress immodestly because they're afraid they won't bag a guy if they don't compete. Nothing could be further from the truth. In seeking a power they think exists, they actually forfeit the power of allure God created within them.

Rather than fearing the possible inability to attract guys, maybe we should fear God. Do you know that the Hebrew word for fear actually means to submit? It means we do things His way, rather than our way—His way, rather than the world's way. And His way is the modest way. His promise couldn't be clearer: "Fear the Lord, you his saints, for those who fear him lack nothing." When we are in line with God's desires for us, we find we have all we need.

{ ♥ **IN YOUR JOURNAL TODAY** . . . Write out your commitment to submit to God's plan regarding finding your dream guy. Just write a letter declaring your intention to follow His plan and then sign it.

HIS
WAY,
RATHER
THAN THE
WORLD'S
WAY.

WEEK 1
THE POWER

DAY 5

Read Genesis 24

{ [Rebekah] took her veil and covered herself. Genesis 24:65

IRONICALLY, THE WORLD'S RESPONSE TO THE MOST SENSUAL STUFF IS NOT WHAT YOU'D THINK. Take, for instance, all this "sexy" reality TV. The sexier the shows, the faster they tank sometimes.

Yet while audiences don't respond all that well to the most sensual reality programming, the reality shows about dating and marriage have experienced skyrocketing success. Now, mind you, most of these shows are also pretty crass, but their success reminds us how much people, deep down, long for romance and true love more than cheap sexual thrills.

I pick up a teen fashion magazine from time to time just to stay fresh with the temptation you face in the worlds of fashion and guys. Get this advice from the liberal mag: "If he's into you, he'll call." It goes on to advise that you calling him only makes him want you less. Even the most out-of-whack magazines of the day agree. It pays to be the girl who waits.

For a better read, feast on the stories you find in the Bible. The Old Testament character of Rebekah must have known about the power of allure, or she was simply obeying the preferences of her parents or of an extremely modest culture. But she didn't rush to Isaac and gush all over him. She covered herself. She let him do the chasing—and chase he did! He married her. The Bible says he later prayed over her when she couldn't have any children. In a society where childbearing was one of the few values of women, he didn't go out and find another wife. He prayed over his dearly loved Rebekah. I find that very romantic. And even when he was an older guy, he was afraid that her extreme beauty might be his undoing. He thought someone might kill him to have her. He never stopped feeling, "Wow!" He had it bad!

Are you looking for power? It comes in resting. Rest in God. He knows your heart. He knows the guys out there, and that makes Him a great matchmaker! Want a great example as to how to attract the perfect mate? Look to women like Rebekah, and you'll have a positive example to follow!

♥ **IN YOUR JOURNAL TODAY** ... Today, we don't wear veils as fashion statements. So look deep into your heart and spend some time journaling about how you might figuratively veil your beauty in a modest way. Would it include not calling guys? Not saying "I love you" too soon? Holding out on kissing? What do you think "veiling" one's beauty means today?

ARE YOU
LOOKING FOR
POWER?
REST IN
GOD.

The **Evolution** } A Decision to Make

THERE USED TO BE A MAJOR DIFFERENCE between women who were considered strippers or porn stars and models. But these days "glamour models" has become the industry's mainstream language for girls who take off their clothes with "class." Now there's no need for such behavior to be kept a secret; taking off your clothes will just make you famous!

If you want to be like these "famous" women, it's easy! I can quickly give you the recipe for their "success" in this week's devotions. The girl who gets all the attention she wants is exactly who the author of Proverbs 7 was studying. You can become like her by taking your cue from the chapter.

YOU JUST HAVE TO DO FIVE THINGS:

1 Come to him dressed like a prostitute (verse 10).

2 Talks too much (verses 11, 21).

3 Kiss him (verse 13).

4 Take him to your room (verses 16, 17).

5 Be alone with him (verse 19).

You might be saying, "Wait! I don't want this kind of famous! Gross!" (Good response.) But here's a hard truth: Many of the well-meaning Christian girls I know don't want to be like the loose woman described in Proverbs 7, but they live like them in these five areas. We're going to take this week to look at Proverbs 7 and dissect the way you live your life to see if it might come dangerously close! If it's okay with you, I want you to read this passage right now.

HERE'S HOW **THE MESSAGE** PARAPHRASES
PROVERBS 7:6–27.

As I stood at the window of my house
looking out through the shutters,
Watching the mindless crowd stroll by,
I spotted a young man without any sense
Arriving at the corner of the street where she lived,
then turning up the path to her house.
It was dusk, the evening coming on,
the darkness thickening into night.
Just then, a woman met him—
she'd been lying in wait for him, dressed to seduce him.
Brazen and brash she was,
restless and roaming, never at home,
Walking the streets, loitering in the mall,
hanging out at every corner in town.

13-20 She threw her arms around him and kissed him,
boldly took his arm and said,
"I've got all the makings for a feast—
today I made my offerings, my vows are all paid,
So now I've come to find you,
hoping to catch sight of your face—and here you are!
I've spread fresh, clean sheets on my bed,
colorful imported linens.
My bed is aromatic with spices
and exotic fragrances.
Come, let's make love all night,
spend the night in ecstatic lovemaking!
My husband's not home; he's away on business,
and he won't be back for a month."

²¹⁻²³ Soon she has him eating out of her hand,
bewitched by her honeyed speech.
Before you know it, he's trotting behind her,
like a calf led to the butcher shop,
Like a stag lured into ambush
and then shot with an arrow,
Like a bird flying into a net
not knowing that its flying life is over.

²⁴⁻²⁷ So, friends, listen to me,
take these words of mine most seriously.
Don't fool around with a woman like that;
don't even stroll through her neighborhood.
Countless victims come under her spell;
she's the death of many a poor man.
She runs a halfway house to hell,
fits you out with a shroud and a coffin.

💜 **SHE'S "THE DEATH OF MANY A POOR MAN"? HIS LIFE IS OVER?** Does that seem drastic? Not really. The Bible says a man's life is ruined by lack of discipline and a guy that cannot say no to a girl like this is definitely in for some hurt. Let's make sure you're not the girl who brings it.

This week, I'm going to ask you five questions relating to what you just read. Let's see if you're a Proverbs 7 woman or something much better! (Let's hope for the second one, but be ready to roll up your sleeves when needed! We all have a little Proverbs 7 in us.)

WHAT DOES SK SAY?

"Blushing is good. Find our why in Chapter 2 of *Secret Keeper*."
—Dannah Gresh

DAY 1

Read Ephesians 5:22–31

{ Then out came a woman to meet him, dressed like a prostitute and with crafty intent. . . . she said: . . . "I came out to meet you; I looked for you and have found you!" Proverbs 7:10, 13, 15

DO YOU THINK GIRLS SHOULD ASK GUYS OUT?

The general consensus today is "yes." I recently monitored an online conversation, and almost every person expressed that it was okay for the girl to be the initiator in a relationship. One writer chimed in, "The time is past when a guy has to be the aggressor—and good riddance!"

What do you think? Should a girl be, as this person calls it, "the aggressor"?

Come on. Make a decision. Draw a line. Circle an answer below.

Okay, with that answer under your belt, let me tell you that there is nowhere in the Bible where a girl is told specifically, "Thou shalt not ask a guy out." So why is there an old-fashioned notion by some in the Church that you should wait for a guy to make the first move?

Here's the biggest reason: God has placed men in authority over women to be their protectors and sacrificial providers. Did you read Ephesians 5? Who's got it harder? The wife? It says submit to and honor this amazing man. Or the husband? It says he should die for her! Clearly, the guy has a harder and more sacrificial task, but girls today get all hotheaded about the fact that we're supposed to honor and let him lead! My pastor once said that God commands women to submit because it's the hardest thing for them in all their speedy self-sufficiency to do. And he calls men to love selflessly because it's that hardest thing for them in all their strength and tough-talk to do.

Through my college years, I feasted on the writings of Elisabeth Elliot, who once wrote:

A real woman understands that man was created to be the initiator, and she operates on that premise. This is primarily a matter of attitude. I am convinced that the woman who understands and accepts with gladness the difference between masculine and feminine will be, without pretense or self-consciousness, womanly.[2]

If you start leading the relationship from the beginning, at what point do you suddenly reverse roles so you can be in the pattern of relationship that God desires? It's not easy to embrace the idea of letting him lead. It will be in stark contrast to the celebs of today—and in contrast to a lot of your friends. The fact is, most teen girls today have no problem being the ones to come out to meet a guy (being the aggressor), dressed in scanty clothing with intentions that are not wholesome. They look a whole lot more like Proverbs 7 women than the Proverbs 31 women we are called to become.

Which will you dare to be?

💙 **IN YOUR JOURNAL TODAY** . . . If you circled "yes" in the options above, take some time to ask God what He thinks about this. If I'm wrong, find some biblical evidence to back up your idea. If I'm right, ask God to soften your heart.

If you circled "no" in the options above, take some time to write out the blessings that may come along with conforming to His plan.

PROVERBS 7 OR
PROVERBS 31:
WHICH
WOMAN
WILL YOU
DARE TO BE?

DAY 2

Read Psalm 37:4–11

{ She is loud and defiant.
Proverbs 7:11

DO YOU TALK TOO MUCH?

It's been hotly debated whether women say more words in a day than men. The widest span I've ever seen came from a CNN interview with Alan Peace that claimed women speak on average 22,000 words a day and men only clock in at 8,000. The closest I've ever seen it is that women speak just over 16,000 words a day, while men come in slightly under that figure.

Either way, women talk more than men do. But that's not really what this verse in Proverbs is saying. It's not how much you talk, but what you say and how you say it that makes you a Proverbs 7 chick.

Various Bible versions of Proverbs 7 use these words to describe her: boisterous, rebellious, loud, stubborn, clamorous, willful, unmanageable. It describes a woman who is proud of who she is, self-reliant, and difficult to control. There's no meekness to be seen. This is a strong woman, the stuff today's protagonists are made of. A recent *USA Today* article described the change in movie heroines from "damsels in distress" to "tomboy sex symbols, women with delicate features who can disarm a tough guy equally as well with a sultry look or a kick to the throat."[3]

That seems to be the goal of the average woman today: to be strong enough to control a guy with both force and seduction. But God uses a very different word for strength in the Scriptures. It is—grasp this—*meekness*. This is a word used to refer to evidence of our progress in growth. You read about it in Psalm 37. "The meek will inherit the land and enjoy great peace" (Psalm 37:11). And in this passage—where David is pleading with God for victory over his enemies—we are called to meekness as a form of strength. It may seem like an improper weapon of strength. But God says His thoughts are not ours, and the weapons we fight with are not the usual weapons of warfare. We are called to be meek—humble, patient, and kind.

The Proverbs 7 woman shows up as the leading lady in most of today's movies. She's dressed in black spandex bodysuits and is able to take out a guy with sensual language or rebellion. But God calls us to dress modestly, speak softly, and show kindness. And that's a role that can carry you through all of life.

❤ **IN YOUR JOURNAL TODAY** . . . Are you easily angered? Do you make sure your voice is heard at a party? Are you impatient with your friends? Are you stubborn? Do you rebel against your parents? Are you constantly critical? If you answered yes to any of these, there's a tad of Proverbs 7 in you. (Relax! There's some in most of us. I feel pretty convicted writing about this.) Take some time today to ask God to give you a heart to obey Him in meekness. Write out your prayers!

WE ARE
CALLED TO
MEEKNESS
AS A FORM OF
STRENGTH.

DAY 3

{ Her feet never stay at home.
Proverbs 7:11

Read Ephesians 6:1–3

DO YOU SPEND ENOUGH TIME AT HOME?

Life calls. Friends text an invitation to come on over. Someone Facebooks an all-call to hang out downtown. There's a big game and everyone who is anyone will be there. Before you know it, you can get to the end of the week and you've only been home long enough to brush your teeth and plop your head onto your pillow.

Allow me to make the case that this could be a dangerous practice.

Proverbs 7 declares that a woman with ill-intent is one whose "feet never stay at home." She's not content; she's looking for the next fix to make her feel important, pretty, needed, sexy, happy, or wanted.

But the Bible calls you to "honor your father and mother." That's something you can do at school as you attain great discipline, at church as you build great character, and with friends as you exercise godly wisdom. Agreed. But it very rarely happens in a haphazard, overly busy hunger to be out of the house.

How can you know the difference?

Brace yourself for this insight! You know the difference by the order of your life at home. Is your bed made? (Or do you forget how that one-minute task works? Come on. It's one minute!) Is your laundry done? (Or piled high on the floor where you sort through it searching for the least-disgusting something to wear each day?) Does your room look like a hurricane has been through it? (Or is it in relative order?) Are you helpful with home chores? (Or do you run away when it's time to do the dishes?) Is your relationship with your parents open and honest? (Or do you give them the silent treatment and run to your laptop for conversation with friends?)

You *can* spend time away from home, but the Proverbs 7 woman is "*never* at home." Are you that girl?

The Proverbs 7 woman wasn't living with her mom and dad; she was living with her husband. And she was still running from home. It makes me wonder if she didn't learn those habits when she was seventeen? Maybe they just stuck. And she kept running from home for the action. How you live today will inform how you live in the future.

Be careful.

♥ **IN YOUR JOURNAL TODAY** . . . I probably stepped on some toes today. Were they yours? I hope not, but if so please know that the Lord loves you like crazy even if your room is messy! But He does want you to learn the value of being at home and building the relationships within it. In your journal, write about what aspect of building relationships in your home that you need to improve upon.

HOW
YOU LIVE
TODAY
WILL
INFORM
HOW YOU
LIVE IN THE
FUTURE.

{ She took hold of him and kissed him. Proverbs 7:13

DO YOU MAKE THE FIRST MOVE WHEN IT COMES TO KISSING?

Kissing is good—very good. It's so good that it quickens your pulse to one hundred beats a minute. It's so good that a soft little kiss will burn three calories! It's so good that men who kiss their wives each morning live an average of five years longer than men who don't! The science of kissing even has its own scientific term: philematology. In my assessment of great movie kisses, I dubbed the sweetest kiss on film to be that between Lady and the Tramp! (Well, at least it was the sauciest!)[4]

But just because kisses can be sweet and saucy—or make you live longer—I don't think you're supposed to go kissing every boy you come into contact with. It is clearly the way of the Proverbs 7 woman to be the physical pursuer in a relationship. Since we don't want to be like her—remember she helps lead a guy to the "chambers of death" (Proverbs 7:27)—we have to believe that it's just better if a girl doesn't act so desperate.

But then there's Song of Songs. This book shows lovers running rampant in tantalizing playful sexual antic. And it all starts with a kiss. "Let him kiss me with the kisses of his mouth—for your love is more delightful than wine!" Clearly, this woman is making known her desires. She wants a kiss. Within the confines of a great, holy marriage, a woman can be playfully pursuant and still be modest and appropriate and fun! But check it out: She doesn't say, "*I* kiss him." She says, "*He* kisses me!" Within marriage she is playful to invite the kissing, but she still lets him initiate the actual physical contact.

I don't think my theology of philematology is going to make or break your spiritual life. So argue with me if you have a difference of opinion in what you're seeing here. Invite in wiser scholars. Dissect my supposition. I'm okay with that. I could be wrong.

But I do know this: It feels good to be kissed. Even better than kissing my man after a long day away is the fact that he walks over and chooses to plant one on me! His intention warms my heart beyond imagination. The Proverbs 7 woman was too busy to ever really find out what it feels like to be chosen. The chick in Song of Songs did.

Don't you want to know the beauty of being chosen?

♥ **IN YOUR JOURNAL TODAY** . . . Write out a defending argument for letting the guy be the physical pursuer—or for being that yourself, if that's what you think is right. Ask yourself why you believe what you believe. Is your argument based on what you *feel* or on what you read and reason through your reading of scripture? Be sure to give this to God in prayer as you journal!

THE BEAUTY
OF BEING
CHOSEN

DAY 5

Read Genesis 24:1–58

{ I have covered my bed with colored linens from Egypt. I have perfumed my bed with myrrh, aloes, and cinnamon. . . . My husband is not at home. Proverbs 7:16–17, 19

CAN YOU BE ALONE WITH A GUY?

Since I worked on my first book, *And the Bride Wore White*, I've been trying to convince teen girls everywhere to "stay public" and to "stay vertical." I believe that being alone with a guy breaks down all your defenses.

Despite this fact, it has become common for a girl to take a guy to her bedroom and lay on the bed with him. Maybe they're "just" checking out Facebook on her laptop together. Perhaps they're "just" giving each other a massage. Or "just" sharing the deepest darkest secrets of their heart. And often this is happening when the house is completely empty, the parents are not at home! (Can you say sexual tension?)

Being alone is a recipe for disaster.

The Proverbs 7 woman is always eager to get a guy into her house alone and to make the bed comfy for him. (Okay, I do know her intentions were pretty clear. But sometimes our intentions to stay pure can be squashed by sexual tension when we get alone.)

In contrast, our Bible reading today shares the story of a strong woman—strong enough to haul up gallons of water for several camels when one thirsty camel can drink up to twenty-five gallons at a time! This young woman stayed under the wise protection and covering of her family. The families—not Rebekah and Isaac—led the way in protecting the virtue of the couple-to-be.

A wise woman is not alone in her pursuit of a guy but surrounded by a full house of family. In this way, she keeps the deepest secrets of her beauty for just one man.

{ ❤ **IN YOUR JOURNAL TODAY** ... Confess to the Lord anything you've been doing to hinder your ability to live a pure, modest life. Ask God for strength to begin to save the deepest secrets of your beauty for just one man.

DIG
DEEPER
INTO
PROVERBS 7
WITH MARY
KASSIAN'S
BOOK **GIRLS
GONE WISE**,
WHICH OFFERS
AN ATTRACTIVE
CONTRAST
TO "GIRLS
GONE WILD."

3

The Secret } A Challenge to Consider: Truth or Bare?

OKAY, IT'S TIME TO THINK! We are not repressed, unintelligent girls; we are women of God with well-thought-out standards. There's a lot of temptation for us to bare it all just like the rest of the world does, and we need a good dose of solid truth to arm us against the seduction.

We need to think about the term *sexy*. A recent animal rights ad suggests that pasta and vegetables can be sexy. (The definition of *sexy* is "to be sexually suggestive or stimulating; attractive." If pasta and vegetables are creating that kind of reaction in people, then—well, let's not go there!)

SEXY HAIR brand shampoo promises a sexy look. (Does this apply if I happen to use their shampoo on my dog? Incidentally, 29 percent of *InStyle* magazine readers say dogs are sexy. Somehow, I think I'd feel more comfortable if they thought pasta and vegetables were sexy.)

Doritos sure seem sexy, according to their famous Super Bowl commercials featuring a scantily clad woman catching them between her teeth. (Gee, the last time I crunched down a bag, I just got bad breath and orange fingers!) Please forgive my sarcasm, but CAN YOU SEE HOW SILLY "SEXY" CAN BE SOMETIMES?

I recently had the privilege of sitting under the teaching of world-renowned evangelist Ravi Zacharias. He spent much of his time that night talking about the world's constant pull to undress women. He explained that a recent court case argued for the pornographic exposure of women, stating that it was merely art. One lawyer argued that much as we view the female body disrobed in an art gallery, we can also view it disrobed in other places. He said that these are equal goods. Is that true? Is the pornography so prevalently available on the Internet merely art? Does nudity equal art?

Zacharias went on: Suppose you have a cow. That cow has many bodily secretions. One of them is milk. Another is urine. Do you see these as equals? They are both excrements. Certainly the logical conclusion is that they are neutral substances of equal value, right? Of course not! Milk is an excretion made for nutrition. We consume it because it is wholesome, naturally good for us. Urine is meant for discarding. It has no relevant use. To use it as we would milk would be vulgar and repulsive.

Don't be fooled into this world's mind-set. You cannot believe that a woman's disrobing, whether it is in a fashion magazine or a porn magazine, ever has a relevant public use. God created your secret beauty to be just that—a secret to be romantically shared with your husband. In that setting, taking your clothes off is for your good and for your emotional and physical pleasure. In any other setting, taking one's clothes off has been robbed of its goodness and cannot fulfill God's intended use for your beauty.

Dive with me a little deeper this week as we begin to unmask some of the lies of this world concerning your beauty and modesty. We're going to consider how we might treat your sexy side as a precious secret to be saved for just one man.

💜 **GOD CREATED YOUR SECRET BEAUTY TO BE JUST THAT—A SECRET TO BE ROMANTICALLY SHARED WITH YOUR HUSBAND.**

WHAT DOES SK SAY?

"Ever since Eve, guys have been glancing. Oh, have they been glancing! Find out why in chapter 3 of *Secret Keeper.*"
—Dannah Gresh

{ Adam lay [yada] with his wife Eve, and she became pregnant and gave birth to Cain. Genesis 4:1

DON'T BE SURPRISED BY THIS, BUT I BELIEVE GOD CREATED YOU TO BE SEXY. I just don't think that the world's casual use of *sexy* means the same thing as God's definition of it.

The Bible's Hebrew word for sex is *yada*. When the Bible says, "Adam lay [yada] with his wife," the word means "knew, recognized, understood, respected." The word is used both in reference to a man and wife having sexual intercourse and—get this—in reference to a person being in deep fellowship with God. The book of Ephesians compares God's relationship with us to marriage (Ephesians 5). This is a great mystery. But when our marriage relationships are pure and free from sexual sin, they have so much intense passion in them that they are the closest thing on this earth God can use to help us understand His passion for us. That's pretty intense stuff!

Sexy is the adjective form of sex. That means, in God's eyes, sexy is when you are known intimately, recognized to the core of your being for who you are, understood (perhaps without even the need to explain yourself), and deeply respected. Do you see that reflected in today's cheap imitation of sexy?

Of course, God does include the physical appeal that the world defines as sexy within His precious Word. Proverbs 5:18–19 says, "Rejoice in the wife of your youth. A loving doe, a graceful deer—may her breasts satisfy you always, may you ever be captivated by her love." That verse acknowledges that we have the power to be captivating, or better translated, "intoxicating." But take a look at how many women the guy in Proverbs is intoxicated by: just the one—the wife of his youth.

When you put the definition of *yada* together with this verse about intoxicating your husband, you'll discover that there are deep secrets about you that only your husband is supposed to know. God did create you to be sexy, but not this world's cheap compromise of sexy. When you choose to be sexy for only your husband, you live according to God's purpose—and rather than losing respect, you gain it.

♥ **IN YOUR JOURNAL TODAY . . .** Write the definition of *yada* in your journal. This is such a powerful word. Never forget it! Now, consider what this meant in Adam and Eve's love relationship. What emotional and spiritual connection do you think they experienced?

DIG DEEPER
INTO THE WORD **YADA** WITH MY BOOK FOR OLDER TEENS, **WHAT ARE YOU WAITING FOR?**: THE ONE THING NO ONE EVER TELLS YOU ABOUT SEX.

REVISE YOUR DEFINITION OF SEXY — GOD'S WAY!

{ Sixty queens there may be, and eighty concubines, and virgins beyond number; but my dove, my perfect one, is unique. Song of Songs 6:8–9

HER SISTERS CALLED HER MOLE FACE. She was terribly self-conscious of the small, perfectly round, brown birthmark to the left of her mouth. It seemed like a horrible thing. Yet when she was sixteen a local newspaper photographer took a photo of her shucking some corn. The rest was history. Cindy Crawford is credited as having changed the role of supermodel. She's been featured on more than four hundred magazine covers and is considered one of the most beautiful women alive.

And she still has her mole. In fact, it is considered the trademark of her beauty.

Why is it that we spend most of our teen years worrying about how different we look from everyone else? The author of Song of Solomon defined real beauty for us when he wrote, "My dove, my perfect one, is unique" (6:8–9). Real beauty is made up of that which makes us distinctly different from everyone else.

I spent most of my teen years obsessing that my eyes weren't wide enough. My brother had long, dark eyelashes, and I had wimpy short ones. I just knew that if God had created my eyes just a little wider, a little bluer, a little, then I'd be more beautiful.

Do you know one of the first things I ever remember my husband telling me during our dating years in college? He said my eyes were beautiful! I could hardly believe it! Was it possible God hadn't made a mistake in making them just as they are?

God crafted you. You are a masterpiece by the finest artist there ever was. He molded your nose to be exactly as it is. He chose the color of your hair. He chiseled your bones, giving you your structure. He even developed the sound of your voice. Psalm 139 tells us He "knit" you together, that you were "woven together." The term used here, *raqan*, was used by skilled embroiderers. We're talkin' a one-of-a-kind piece of art—every strand carefully selected, every color perfectly placed.

God crafted you.

What makes you feel unique? Do you realize that just might turn out to be your beauty mark?

♥ **IN YOUR JOURNAL TODAY** . . . Write a letter to God, pouring out to Him the parts of you that make you feel unusually different. Go ahead and cry about it, if it happens to be that kind of day. It's okay. We're girls; we do that. But can I encourage you to end with some praising?

GOD
CRAFTED
YOU.

WEEK 3
THE SECRET

DAY 3

Read 1 Peter 3:1–7

{ Your beauty should not come from outward adornment, such as braided hair and the wearing of gold jewelry and fine clothes. Instead, it should be that of your inner self, the unfading beauty of a gentle and quiet spirit, which is of great worth in God's sight. 1 Peter 3:3–4

ONE SAN FRANCISCO FIFTEEN-YEAR-OLD CONFESSED to *U.S. News & World Report* that if she's "had a good shopping day" she "feels kind of beautiful." She says her Coach purse is her "prized possession." Good grief!

And yet I can identify with that girl. I've shopped to soothe a broken heart before. I've experienced what I call "post-purchase dissonance"—that really bad feeling you get after you spend too much on something you "just had to have." (Oh, you know what I'm talking about, huh? Well, now you know what to call it!)

I'd like to think I'm far less shallow than that fifteen-year-old girl, but if I let myself get too far from the true source of my beauty, I'm not all that different.

Can you identify?

So what is the true source of your beauty? First Peter 3:3–4 says it's not fancy clothes. It's not a great new haircut. It's not even marvelous jewelry.

Your true beauty lies inside. It's the gentle, quiet spirit that God creates in you when you get alone with Him and let Him make you into who He desires you to be.

So how do you know if you're letting God do that? Well, I like to start each morning with ABC (The Absolute Beauty Challenge!). You can do it, too. Here's how:

First find your ABC note card. When you do this, write on it the amount of time you intend to spend with God every morning. (Hint: Since we want our inside to be more beautiful than our outside, the time should be MORE than we spend in front of the mirror coifing our do!) If it takes you twenty minutes to get beautified each morning, you might want to aim for spending twenty-five minutes with God! See how it works?

Tape the ABC note card to your bathroom mirror.

Then ask yourself each and every morning, "Did I spend more time in God's Word than I spent in front of this mirror?"

This should be easy during our thirty-day plunge, but keep that card up there. The rubber meets the road in the weeks to come!

♥ **IN YOUR JOURNAL TODAY** . . . Rather than responding by writing today, take a few moments to get that note card out and post it on your mirror. If you're studying this book with a group of friends, why not call one of them and tell her what your time goal with God is. Ask her if she's posted her **A**bsolute **B**eauty **C**hallenge yet!

START
EACH
MORNING
WITH
ABC!

{ But I tell you that anyone who looks at a woman lustfully has already committed adultery with her in his heart. Matthew 5:28

HAVE YOU SEEN THE MOVIE *THE NOTEBOOK*? In it an old man reads the journal of a young lover to an old woman who has Alzheimer's and has lost all memory of her former life. The story is amazingly romantic.

He's poor.

She's rich.

Theirs is a summer love.

It's opposed by her parents.

Years pass.

The love doesn't fade.

As adults, they later wed just before it's too late—just before she's about to marry a more refined, high-profile man.

It's wild and free and romantic.

The heartbreaker is that he's reading to her from her own journal.

They are the young lovers—only she can't remember except for brief moments when the notebook he's reading from takes her to a place where her heart supersedes her mind and she loves him back.

The Notebook is a really romantic film, isn't it? But I confess to you that though I viewed it innocently the first time I saw it, I could not view it again without it being sin. It would be pornography to my heart. There are two vivid sexual scenes in the movie that would take my heart to places it has no right being without my body—and my husband!

How's your own emotional purity?

Bathsheba's wasn't too great, and she ended up committing adultery and getting pregnant. Emotional impurity is just the first step toward more horrible sin. Jesus said that men who looked at women lustfully had already committed sexual sin in their hearts. Is it any different when we, as women, clearly and purposefully dress ourselves and place ourselves in the field of vision to receive that lust?

And sometimes we do.

Bathsheba did.

How's your emotional purity?

{ ♥ IN YOUR JOURNAL TODAY . . . Write Matthew 5:28 out in your journal, and then recall a time when you knew in your heart you were setting yourself up to be viewed just as Bathsheba did. Ask God to forgive you and to shield you from emotional impurity. If you cannot recall such a time, simply praise Him and continue to walk in innocence!

HOW'S
YOUR
EMOTIONAL
PURITY?

{ They [God's people] mingled with the nations and adopted their customs . . . therefore the Lord was angry. Psalm 106:35, 40

REMEMBER THAT WONDERFUL WORD WE EXPLORED A FEW DAYS AGO? *Yada!* It meant "to know, to be known, to be deeply respected." It's God's word for sex.

While we're examining the truth about being bare this week, let's look a little more deeply at how precious this word is by studying its opposite. You see, the world is constantly feeding us so many sexual messages it is easy to presuppose that all sex is the same. We naturally imagine the sex we will enjoy with our husbands one day is like the sex portrayed on TV shows. On one recent program—which I didn't watch myself but heard about—a teen had sex with the mother of his ex-girlfriend. Later he explored homosexual relationships.

Is this *yada*?

No. It's *sakab.* This word appears in Genesis 19:33 when "the older daughter went in and lay [sakab] with [her dad]." Yuck! What does *sakab* mean? It means "to exchange bodily emissions." It's a mere physical exchange of body fluid.

Obviously, not all sex is the same.

Remember the difference in your quest to discover the truth about sex. What you see on popular television shows isn't God's plan for your sexual life. This makes me wonder, should we be watching those programs at all? Psalm 106:35 describes how God's people mingled with the nations and adopted their customs, despite God's clear instructions to His people to maintain their purity. That's kind of what happens when we feed on the world's ways. We eventually end up accepting them.

Don't accept a mixed-up message about God's precious gift of your body. It's far too valuable!

Let's stop feeding ourselves messages about *sakab* so that we are untainted and can truly know *yada*!

♥ **IN YOUR JOURNAL TODAY** ... Think back over the past twenty-four hours. How many images of *sakab* did you see? Posters? Television shows? Magazines? People at school? Think hard. List them all. Now ask yourself if there were any of those images you could have avoided? If so, ask God to help you be more faithful to protect your eyes.

YADA!
IT'S GOD'S WORD!

4

The **Mark** } A Father's Thoughts

LEXI, MY SPUNKY AND BEAUTIFUL, FRECKLE-LADEN, BRIGHT-EYED BRUNETTE, has a really amazing daddy, whose creativity blesses me on birthdays, anniversaries, and holidays.

She's had three very special birthdays and will have one more before she is released by her daddy to get married. I've had nothing to do with it. When she was nine she wrote this:

> **When I was 5 my dad gave me a special gift. It was a small heart-shaped box made of metal and inside it was a golden bracelet with blue gems in it. On the bottom of the box it said,**
>
> **"To Lexi From Daddy**
> **December 28, 1998**
> **Something Blue"**
>
> **When I turn 10, 15, and 20 I'll get "Something Old," "Something New," or "Something Borrowed" for my birthday. The next one will be for my 10th birthday. Once I get all of them I'll use them at my wedding. It makes me feel special to get these gifts. They are beautiful.**

IS THAT ROMANTIC OR WHAT? On her tenth birthday Lexi received "Something Old," a silver chain with a tiny silver heart studded with a diamond chip. The chip was my grandmother's engagement diamond nearly seventy years ago. It was placed into the necklace and given as a gift to my mother when her daddy died. It's a very special "Something

Old." For her fifteenth birthday, Lexi got a "Something New"—a handkerchief handcrafted with her name. The edging is trimmed with lace handmade by a relative.

{ SOMETHING NEW

A father's heart is one of the deepest reservoirs of romance that you can ever know.

Oops! I just lost some of you, huh?

Got a dad you can't seem to get along with? One who's gone, maybe? Or one who's consumed with his own life? Open your Bible to Psalm 68:5–6. It says, "A father to the fatherless, a defender of widows, is God in his holy dwelling. God sets the lonely in families."

I hope you have an earthly father like Lexi's dad—my sweet and romantic husband. His tender commitment to directing her toward a good and perfect gift of sexuality is priceless. God desires this kind of parenting investment.

This week, we're going to explore how your Father God is protective, jealous, firm, and provisional. Just as Lexi's daddy is making some strong statements about guys in her early years, so does the Father in heaven have a lot to say to you about guys!

♥ ARE YOU BOY-CRAZY?
GET READY TO GET GOD-CRAZY!

WHAT DOES SK SAY?

"Buckle up, if you dare! Chapter 4 of *Secret Keeper* takes you into the minds of guys!"
—Dannah Gresh

WEEK 4
THE MARK

DAY 1

Read Genesis 2:15–25

{ For this reason a man will leave his father and mother and be united to his wife, and they will become one flesh. The man and his wife were both naked, and they felt no shame. Genesis 2:24–25

TOUCHING YOUR HUSBAND RELEASES A CHEMICAL IN THE BRAIN CALLED OXYTOCIN THAT IS KIND OF LIKE GLUE. What an odd fact, huh?

The warmth and intimacy of a husband and wife holding one another naked is comforting like nothing I've ever known in my entire life. (This is *yada*, not *sakab*. Remember those words from last week?) In fact, there's really not anything sexual about those moments. They are safe, warming, and sometimes even healing.

Shameless oneness. That's what my husband calls nakedness between a husband and a wife.

This future relationship that God has planned for you is fantastic, but He has designed it to work a certain way. He's created you to be in shameless oneness with just one man.

Not many men. That's "the mark"—the bull's-eye you should aim for. God wants you to save yourself for just one man.

No matter what Hollywood tells you, it does not work to be in intimate relationships with many men. You know the result of that kind of life? Depression. The suicide rate among sexually active teenage girls is six to twelve times higher than their virgin peers. Those same girls are more likely to be anorgasmic (unable to climax sexually) in marriage. Their attempts to have lots of pleasure end up in a lot less enjoyment. On the contrary, even some of today's most liberal sexual studies state that those who did not engage in premarital sex report higher levels of sexual satisfaction—and those who engage in sex most frequently are the middle-aged, married couples with happy friendships. God wants this for you!

Do you ever wonder why God didn't just create Adam and Eve at the same time and plop them together? I do. One reason may be that He delights in presenting one man to one woman. He did it carefully with Adam and Eve; will you let Him do it in His care and timing with you?

Until then, it is your job to be faithfully waiting. Are you?

❤ **IN YOUR JOURNAL TODAY** . . . In your journal, I want you to do one of two things. If you've never been in a significant dating relationship with your heart or body involved, I want you to write a letter of commitment to your Father in heaven. Tell Him you want to wait for Him to bring you into shameless oneness and you don't want to miss His timing. If you have had your heart or your body broken by relationships, first confess these to the Father in heaven. Then recommit yourself to a life of purity.

HIT THE BULL'S-EYE.

DAY 2

Read Ephesians 5:22–33

{ But among you there must not be even a hint of sexual immorality, or of any kind of impurity, or of greed, because these are improper for God's holy people. Ephesians 5:3

YOU KNOW THOSE BUBBLE-PACKAGED PILLS—the ones where you have to peel the foil backing off the top of the bottle? I find them to be a recipe for frustration! Now you can't even get into a bottle of vitamins without facing a child-safety lid and tamper-proof seal.

The safety-cap obsession really started all the way back in 1982. That was the year of the Tylenol murders. Someone apparently opened the bottles, laced the pills with cyanide, and allowed them to be placed on the shelves for sale. Seven people died. Did they know there was cyanide in or on the pills? No. Did the pills appear to be much different from those that were not dangerous? No. There was just a "hint" of cyanide.

That "hint" reminds me of how many teens today approach sexual sin. It's just some passionate kissing. It's just a little foreplay. How can that be sin? It's just "a little."

Yet God our Father tells us there should not be even a "hint" of sexual sin in our lives. You know that "How far is too far?" question in everyone's mind? Well, there's your answer. Not even a hint!

Let me ask you something. Does a guy hint at sexual sin when he surfs the Net looking for porn? Oh, yes! Does a girl hint at sexual sin when she wears clothes so tight they leave nothing to the imagination? Yep! Does a teen couple hint at sexual sin when they engage in sexual language while chatting on Facebook? What about sexting? Absolutely. To these things God says no!

God your Father has set up the standard for you. It's not just waiting for sexual intercourse until you're married; it's avoiding even a hint of sexual sin.

I hate to even write about this, but I think I have to. A lot of teens today—Christian teens included—think that oral sex is perfectly acceptable. But that hint of sexual sin can result in HPV, the human papillomavirus. It's the fastest-spreading sexually transmitted disease today and is responsible for almost all cervical cancer cases and—get this—is being linked to throat cancer in teens.

Just a hint?

For the sake of your life, just say "no!"

♥ IN YOUR JOURNAL TODAY ... Struggling with oral sex? Think about it and confess that in your journal. If not, I want you to write about whom you can challenge with this information. Maybe it's a friend you know. Maybe you don't have any friends experimenting with their sexuality—yet. But God may provide a friend in the future who needs this information. Ask the Lord to give you courage to be ready to share it.

WATCH OUT
FOR THOSE
DANGEROUS
LITTLE
HINTS!

WEEK 4
THE MARK

DAY 3

Read John 2:1–11

> Daughters . . . I charge you . . . do not arouse or awaken love until it so desires. Song of Songs 2:7

MANY YEARS AGO WHEN I MOVED INTO A NEW HOME, I HAD REALLY, REALLY GOOD INTENTIONS. I'd planned to decorate my living room in honor of the Old Testament tabernacle. No gaudy, tacky, or poorly modeled relics or anything. I just wanted it to be symbolic. The colors would be purple, blue, and red just like the tabernacle, and I'd write Scripture verses on the walls. I got started and made some progress and was about to do the windows when God started nudging me. You see, I'd planned to have an interior designer custom-make my window treatments. That, my friend, would never be done on *Trading Spaces* as it would never fit into the $1,000 per-room budget. Custom-designed treatments are a lavish expense, and God was convicting me that this wasn't a wise use of our money. Did I whine a bit? Yes. Did I wait a bit? I waited a lot! I just got my Spiegel specials a couple of months ago. They were much cheaper, and each time someone praises my new window decor (probably wondering why they were bare for more than three years), my heart leaps with a sense of accomplishment. I waited. I obeyed God. These curtains are a visible reminder for me each day.

In John 2, we see that even Jesus knew He had to wait on His Father's timing. How fitting that it was a wedding at which we see Him vocalize this obedience. Just as He listened to His earthly mother's pleading to begin His public ministry, so He must have taken a moment to approach His heavenly Father. After all, the Word says He only does what He sees or is told to do by His Father.

God our Father cares about timing. He wants to be consulted about every detail of our lives—from how you cover your windows to what pair of jeans you buy to the very, very big decision of when you will allow romantic love to be awakened. God even included a verse just for that one. In Song of Solomon 2:7, He speaks to you and me tenderly as "daughters." He charges us not to awaken or arouse love until the right time. When is the right time? When your parents have released you to date or court. When you know that you are nearing the age when you can be financially and physically independent from them. Don't even play with love until then.

♥ **IN YOUR JOURNAL TODAY** . . . How are you doing in letting love sleep? Are you the girl who's consumed by the latest "hottie," or are you obeying God by allowing those passions to rest for now? Oh, the sense of accomplishment you'll know if you can just wait for the right timing! In your journal, write out Song of Solomon 2:7 as a prayer to God, and tell Him how it makes you feel. Is it painful? Difficult? Comforting? Let your feelings flow to your heavenly Father! **WRITE SONG OF SOLOMON 2:7 OUT AS A PRAYER.**

GOD
OUR
FATHER
CARES
ABOUT
TIMING.

{ Keep my commands and you will live; . . . they will keep you from . . . seductive words. Proverbs 7:2, 5

IT WAS ONE OF THE DUMBEST NIGHTS OF MY LIFE, BAR NONE.

Our family was in South Africa eagerly awaiting our entrance the very next day into the world-famous Mala Mala Game Preserve where we would go on several photo safaris in search of Africa's big five: lions, leopards, elephants, rhinos, and water buffaloes. They are called this because they are the most dangerous of animals to hunt, often turning on the hunter when wounded rather than continuing to run away.

Eager with anticipation, we decided to embark upon our own little safari. We'd heard that the little river where our cabin was located contained hippopotamuses, so we decided to go on a nighttime hippo hunt. We gathered our flashlights and set out along a marshy area in the river.

We heard the hippos. They'd snort or moan. Occasionally one would move in the brush nearby or the water would ripple in the moonlight. Our adrenaline rushed, and we sought more intently. After a lengthy walk, we came to a bridge and turned our flashlights onto a nearby field. There, glistening in the light, was a handful of pudgy hippos munching on grass. As quickly as our light caught their eyes, they raced into the water and submerged.

Gone.

The next day we found out that hippos are the most dangerous land mammals in Africa, often crushing humans. If only I'd read the Kruger Park wildlife guide! If you get to Africa, DO NOT go hunting hippos in the dark, armed with nothing more than a flashlight!

We live like that sometimes—plunging ahead without consulting the guidelines. There are many dangers to us here on this earth. God has given us a guidebook so we can be aware of them. We often fail to read it, and consequently we miss the mark. Not intentionally, but we still miss it.

Proverbs 7:2 says, "Keep my commands and you will live." It doesn't get much clearer than that, does it? The passage goes on to say that the commands will keep us from seductive words, from lust. And if we don't read His Word, we can only hope that He'll come along and discipline us. That night when we were out in the dark looking for hippos, I'd have probably resented a game ranger shooing us back into our cabin, but it would have been a loving gift of protection from God. When we step out of His Word, He often sends discipline to keep us safe (sometimes in the form of parents). Do we appreciate it? Not usually. Let's learn to.

♥ IN YOUR JOURNAL TODAY . . . If you'll take my suggestion, I'd like to choose a verse for you to memorize, one that fits our focus on instructions from the Father. Proverbs 3:12 reads, "The Lord disciplines those he loves, as a father the son he delights in." Write it in your journal and also on a "Thoughts from the Father" card you can put somewhere you can see it so you will commit this verse to memory. His Word is a powerful weapon against lust.

GOD HAS
GIVEN US A
GUIDEBOOK.

{ "You did not choose me, but I chose you and appointed you to go and bear fruit—fruit that will last. Then the Father will give you whatever you ask in my name." John 15:16

MOST GIRLS DREAM OF HAVING BABIES. I've even met some who tell me in wide-eyed passion, "I just want to get married, have babies, and then Jesus can come."

I was the same way myself as a little girl.

Imagine the pain when that dream doesn't come true.

My sweet, beautiful friend Laura is a blonde, hip-as-they-come, twenty-something woman with a passion for Christ like few ever experience. She and her husband, Ryan, spent much of one recent summer grieving the loss of children. Children she'd never had. The doctors had pronounced her infertile with only a 10 percent chance of having children with the strongest of fertility treatments.

She has devoted her life to serving God in many capacities. Why, oh why, would He deny her this pleasure?

After months of struggling, they decided as a couple to wait on God rather than participate in the fertility treatments. Laura began to eat a strict and very healthy natural diet. And she asked God for a baby.

Just weeks after the diagnosis, she was at a Jars of Clay concert when she felt God say, "Reach out your arms and receive your baby boy." She went home and told Ryan, who understandably didn't want her to be hurt if it was not true and told her it might be too soon. She called her doctor, who assured her it could not be true. Her body could not have healed itself so quickly. Still, Laura felt God saying she'd been given a baby.

A few days later, after insistence that she be tested, the doctor announced her miracle. She was, indeed, pregnant. Imagine my contentment with being able to throw her a surprise baby shower.

John 15 tells us that we can, in fact, ask God for the desires of our hearts, and He will answer us. What He looks for in our request is a heart yielded to Him, one deeply connected to Him and His will. Because my friend Laura had a heart like that, God answered this request miraculously.

Do you want the guy of your dreams one day? Bear fruit.

Do you want to have a great family one day? Bear fruit.

Do you want to travel the world and share God's love? Bear fruit.

The deepest dreams of your heart, including the romantic dreams, are things you can ask of the Father. Ask Him, and either He will allow your desires to change because you are so connected to Him . . . or He'll patiently prepare you for the precious answer to your request.

❤ **IN YOUR JOURNAL TODAY** . . . What fruit have you seen in your life? Scribble some ideas. Have you ever helped someone understand salvation through Jesus? Discipled a friend? Given your time to meet the needs of the poor? Given money to help a food shelter? What fruit is in your life? It's not too soon to begin. Won't you sit silently and ask God what fruit He desires for you to bear today? Then, go grow fruit!

THE
DREAMS
OF YOUR
HEART.

5

The Allure } A Vanity Fast

SHE WAS BEAUTIFUL. Sixteen. Long, brown wispy hair. No makeup. Rugged jeans and a simple T-shirt.

I'll never forget her inspiration in my life.

"Dannah," she said, "what you've been talking about—the clothes, the makeup, the modesty—those are all big issues in my life. I really struggle with being overwhelmed with the surface, and I ignore my internal beauty."

"Really?" I asked, surprised. She seemed so down-to-earth and natural.

"This isn't what I usually look like," she confessed. "God told me not long ago to go on a vanity fast. No makeup. No special stuff with my hair, and only jeans and T's except for when I need to honor my parents with the way that I dress. I locked up my jewelry and makeup and trendy little outfits. For one month, it's just me and God! And I'm loving it!"

She inspired me.

And soon God showed me that this vanity fast is not a new idea.

In Exodus 38:8 we find a vanity fast. It says, **"They made the bronze basin and its bronze stand from the mirrors of the women who served at the entrance to the Tent of Meeting."** They were building the temple—the place where they could draw near to the presence of the living God. And nothing could stand in the way. The mirrors the women offered took away their opportunity to be vain. They were out in the desert—no running water, no blow-dryers, no mirrors. I mean, talk about roughing it! Their one luxury for beauty was the mirrors they'd plundered from the Egyptians when they left. These were crude, polished pieces of metal that enabled the women to see their images. In offering them to God, they were giving up their last relics of modern beauty.

{ **PLUNGE WITH ME A FEW FEET FURTHER FROM THE WORLD AND CLOSER TO GOD.**

These mirrors were broken into many pieces and molded together into a basin—a basin that Aaron, the priest, would wash in after he'd sacrificed an animal to God. He would actually be able to see himself in the outer court, the court of God. It was not only a sacrifice of vanity, but it brought them as a people closer to the God who'd rescued them. That's what happens when we get the trappings of this world out of the way. We get closer to God.

Mirrors. Magazines. Television. Movies. Hours in front of the mirror. Spending sprees. These objects and pastimes aren't evil in and of themselves, but when we feast on them too much, they become barriers between us and God. When sacrificed, they become reflective places in which we can see ourselves in His presence.

My friend Janet once fasted from spending any money whatsoever on anything related to beauty, fashion, or vanity. She was amazed at how hard it was and how programmed she was to spend money on useless, vain things. She was also amazed at how rewarded she was with God's presence.

Want a really "wow" experience? Plunge with me a few feet deeper—a few feet further from the world and closer to God.

Plunge with me into a two-week vanity fast.

WHAT'S A VANITY FAST?

So what's a vanity fast? It's fasting from one thing that seems to have a hold on you related to your beauty. It could be excessive spending or just mindless spending on lots of little things. It could be overindulgence in mirror-time. (I had a friend in high school who needed two full hours to get ready every morning!) It could be feeding on fashion magazines. (Got pages plastered all over the walls of your room? Could be a sign that this is the area for fasting for you!) Just ask God to show you what you need to take a break from so you can get closer to Him!

Then make a commitment to remove the influence from your life for fourteen days!

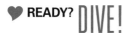 **READY?** DIVE!

 WHAT DOES SK SAY? "Flowers, Valentine's Day gifts, and romantic dinners are some of the ways a man might try to prove himself worthy of your virtue. Find out how modesty works in your favor in *Secret Keeper* chapter 5."
—Dannah Gresh

DAY 1

{ I have seen all the works which have been done under the sun, and behold, all is vanity and striving after wind. Ecclesiastes 1:14 NASB

SHE WAS ONLY SEVENTEEN, and not yet a Christian, when Elite Modeling Agency in New York City discovered her. Kim Alexis was an athlete who spent up to five and a half hours a day swimming and lifting weights as a member of her high school swim team. She was definitely fit.

"By the way, Kim, you have to lose fifteen pounds." Those were her first orders from her new boss once the agency contracted her. Kim was devastated, but she believed the lie he spoke to her. She began to starve herself. She recalls one day sitting down to eat a head of lettuce—the only food she'd had all day. Kim soon graced the cover of over five hundred magazines including *Vogue* and *Sports Illustrated*'s swimsuit issue. She was one of the first true supermodels—and she was miserable. Her body was so stressed that she didn't have her period for two full years. She cried a lot during the first year of her modeling career.

"The constant pressure to look and dress a certain way, to present a certain image, made me feel very insecure and vulnerable," recalls Kim in *Today's Christian Woman*.

Isn't that crazy? The very thing most people would think would bring her a sense of value and beauty actually created insecurity and vulnerability. That's what vanity does!

One of the definitions of vanity is "the lack of usefulness or worth." And that's exactly what many of our attempts at beauty become—useless and worthless.

King Solomon writes an ode to vanity in Ecclesiastes. In the first five chapters, he uses the word sixteen times (NASB). Why? Because he's been down the same road Kim Alexis traveled. No, he didn't starve himself or grace the cover of any magazines. He went down the testosterone version of vanity road. He pursued accomplishments. And in the end he said, "I have seen all the works which have been done under the sun, and behold, all is vanity and striving after wind."

Useless pursuits.

Have you, like Kim—or like me or like most warm-bodied women alive—struggled with your weight? Maybe you've starved yourself like Kim? Lost your period? Perhaps you've made yourself vomit or even harmed yourself in other ways. Let's get that in perspective today. It's USELESS. None of the comfort you are searching for is in these things.

None.

💙 **IN YOUR JOURNAL TODAY** . . . Think for a moment. Is there anything you've been doing to "make" yourself more "beautiful"? Excessive exercise? Binging and purging? Too much tanning? Credit card debt? Are you willing to confess that these are useless, worthless pursuits? Pour out your confession and feelings in writing to the Lord, and THEN talk to an older, wiser woman—maybe your mom— and ask for accountability in overcoming this vanity.

WATCH
OUT FOR
VANITY
ROAD!

DAY 2

Read 2 Kings 17:13–18

{ Don't let anyone look down on you because you are young, but set an example for the believers in speech, in life, in love, in faith and in purity.
1 Timothy 4:12

THINK OF EIGHT GIRLS YOU KNOW who are twelve years old or younger. Little sister? Friends of a little sister? Girls in your church? Write their names below:

_____

_____

_____

_____

_____

_____

_____

_____

Picture the girls in your mind. Are they adorable or what? Now, circle all those who are normally or terribly thin.

Get this! A Harvard University study found that two-thirds of underweight twelve-year-olds think they are fat. Do we girls have body-image issues or what? Why do they struggle like this? Today's models weigh 23 percent less than the average woman. (Guess not much has changed since Kim Alexis was in the modeling industry.)

Why are we back here talking about weight again? Because it's one of the number one lies we feast upon as women. We see the models and think they are the standard. Nothing could be further from the truth.

Adults often speak as if they expect teen girls to struggle with beauty, weight issues, and body image. If I hear one more person say, "Teenagers! What can you expect?" I do promise you will hear me scream, though we may be separated by miles and miles.

God's truth says that YOU are an example to believers. It doesn't say to younger believers. It doesn't say to peers. It simply says that you are an example to believers in speech, life, love, faith, and purity.

So no more excuses. You are armed with truth. You are called to be an example of truthful beauty and purity, not to mimic the ways of this world. In 2 Kings, we find that mimicking the ways of the world is nothing new. The Israelites struggled with it too. And as a result, God removed His presence from them.

Are you hungry for God's presence? Still struggling to get below the surface? Dive in with this vanity fast. I promise that when you separate yourself from this world, His presence will be evident and you'll be an example to all believers.

♥ IN YOUR JOURNAL TODAY ... Let's focus on someone else today. How about those preteen girls you named above? Ask God which one you might pray for and encourage today. Write a prayer for her to know God's truth about her beauty. Then drop her a note. Tell her she's beautiful! Be an example of a believer to her.

YOU ARE
AN **EXAMPLE**
TO BELIEVERS.

{ Turn my heart toward your statutes and not toward selfish gain. Turn my eyes away from worthless things; preserve my life according to your word. Psalm 119:36–37

LONDON TAXI DRIVERS HAVE GREAT MEMORIES. For two full years, they must pass rigorous memory training obstacles in order to become licensed. They must know every tiny alley in the big city of London. As a result, MRI results show that they have an enlarged hippocampus. What's a hippocampus? Well, it's not where hippos learn. Rather, it's the memory center of the adult brain. When exercised, it seems, portions of the brain actually grow.

In Germany, some jugglers who practiced daily for three months seemed to have brain tissue growth in the areas of the visual and motor activity. When they stopped practicing, the brain tissue in those areas receded.

When I was in Africa last year, I was astonished at the memory of my Zambian pupils. Having few books, they grow up in a culture filled with oral tradition and teaching. They can memorize a thirty-minute speech filled with statistics, Bible verses, and references after hearing it just once.

The average Western brain is filled to the core with junk. We can barely memorize a verse, let alone a whole speech filled with verses. I think it's because we've been filled with ads, images, lyrics, and instructions for cell phones, laptops, and iPods, as well as news that's rarely good. Our brains are mush!

That is, unless we exercise our spiritual brain muscles.

Did you know that there are two parts of the brain largely associated with how you feel about God? Spiritual memories and feelings are stored in (1) the deep limbic system located in the center of the brain and (2) the left prefrontal cortex, located behind your forehead. Does exercise increase these? Yep! Buddhist monks, who engage in long and quiet meditation, tend to have larger left prefrontal cortexes and warmer activity in the limbic system. This recent finding is so powerful that Dr. Daniel Amen has dubbed the brain the "hardware of the soul."

Let's not make excuses any longer. Let's build up our spiritual brain muscles by hiding God's Word in our hearts. Psalm 119:36–37 promises that as we fill our hearts with His Word, He'll turn our eyes away from worthless (think: vain) things!

♥ IN YOUR JOURNAL TODAY . . . You probably saw this coming, but I think it'd be a great day to memorize a verse. Grab your vanity fast card. You'll notice it's designed for you to write on it. Write out a treasured verse you've been meaning to hide in your heart. Now begin to do just that. It'd be awesome if you could have it memorized by the end of the week! Hey, I promised we were going deep. No spiritual baby food for you. Remember, you're meant to be an example to believers! Don't cut corners. Go deep!

WHAT'S A
HIPPO
CAMPUS?

{ Speaking the truth in love, we will in all things grow up into him. . . . From him the whole body, joined and held together by every supporting ligament, grows and builds itself up in love. Ephesians 4:15–16

LITTLE, DEER-LIKE IMPALAS roam the African plains so freely that they're called the McDonald's of the wild. They're what lions, leopards, and cheetahs lunch on. I was on the trip of my life—an African safari—when I learned a vital lesson from these gentle creatures. You see, we were in our Land Rover looking for leopards. Leopards were the last of the famous African big five to see on our trip. All we seemed to find were more and more impalas. I was about to give up when, suddenly, a small cluster of the impalas stood alert, ears twitching every which way, noses wiggling. A moment later, a braying sound went out across the plains like an alarm. Soon, all of the impalas we could see—and dozens we could not—were just standing there screaming their little heads off.

"Leopard!" shouted our safari ranger.

I wondered why they weren't running madly.

"It won't have lunch here today," he announced.

He went on to explain that leopards are strong rather than fast. They rely on the element of surprise to overtake their prey. In sounding the alarm all together rather than running every which way, the impalas were sticking together—and surviving.

It made me think of that verse about Satan roaming about as a roaring lion seeking whom he might devour. Certainly, we are his prey and have got to stick together.

Recording artist Rebecca St. James says that one of the main ways she overcomes feelings of inferiority, other than staying in God's presence, is to stick close to godly friends. She says, "You'd think a woman who regularly does photo shoots for magazines and has the benefit of hair and makeup stylists would be able to look at some of those images and think, Well, I look okay in this. I feel good about myself. But I don't. Every single day I struggle with measuring myself against models and actresses, even though so many of these women are unhealthily thin." Her solution? "I've found it's key to have friends and family around who allow me to be honest with them and say, 'I'm really struggling in this area. Pray for me today because I'm obsessing about this.'"

I think she's on to something.

Esther, beautiful enough to woo the king, still needed Mordecai for strength and advice. (Did you read it?) And in Ephesians, we are called to speak truth in love to each other and to be held together and built up by love.

How're ya doin' with this vanity fast? Trembling a bit? First pray about it, then "bray" about it. Just like those little impalas, let someone nearby know you need to be built up in love!

{ ♥ **IN YOUR JOURNAL TODAY** . . . Jot a quick note about whatever it is you're obsessing about. Then call a friend today and tell her what you're obsessing about. Pray together!

CALL A FRIEND!

DAY 5

{ What matters is not your outer appearance —the styling of your hair, the jewelry you wear, the cut of your clothes—but your inner disposition. Cultivate inner beauty, the gentle, gracious kind that God delights in. 1 Peter 3:3–4 (THE MESSAGE)

DURING THE RENAISSANCE, WOMEN STRIVED FOR PALE SKIN. It was the latest trend since women who were wealthier never worked outdoors and therefore had paler skin. In Italy, one scheming woman named Signora Tofana created a face powder made from arsenic, which made women quite pale. She began to sell her poisonous product to women who wanted to do away with their spouses. Six hundred dead husbands later, Tofana was executed and the product was deemed illegal.

We girls can be pretty stupid when it comes to beauty, trying every new fad whether it's meant to work for us or not. I've read magazines that depicted beautiful Asian women who desired to be taller like the Western beauties that the media celebrates. They'd actually undergo excruciating surgeries to elongate their shinbones by just a few inches at best. Many of these surgeries went badly— vain attempts at foolish notions of beauty. These women were created to be beautiful at just their height. (Remember, that which makes us unique is that which makes us beautiful!)

We're not called to try this fad and that trend, which is why it's so important not to be overcome by the world's influences. (And why we're on this vanity fast! How're ya doin'? Keep at it. Start fresh today if you've been struggling!)

First Peter tells us that our beauty doesn't come from a great hairstyle, a fabulous new gold anklet, or even the hottest new low-riders. Nope. Beauty comes from the heart. Those other things are just vain attempts. Do they enhance your beauty? Perhaps.

But check out Sarai (Sarah) in Genesis 12. My, she must have been gorgeous. The Pharaoh noticed her and took her into his palace. (Imagine showing up at a great party in Washington, DC, that the president is NOT at, but days later he hears about your beauty and invites you to the White House!) She was a supermodel of the time. And guess what? God allows His Word to record that she was physically beautiful, but as we see in the 1 Peter passage, the best kind of beauty comes from within.

The Bible doesn't say you can't wear vintage polos or cool shades of eye shadow. It even says that beautiful women like Esther used beauty treatments and cosmetics (Esther 2:9). But the Bible is clear that a beautiful heart and character is what really matters. And that's exactly what we're going to start to work on next week. Ready to go a few feet deeper?

♥ IN YOUR JOURNAL TODAY ... After reading about Sarah, think hard. Meditate on it. Can you see any qualities in Sarah that demonstrated that her beauty came from within? I can. Do you see it too? Submission. (Oh, what an old-fashioned word!) Sarah was loyal and willing to follow her husband and (most importantly) follow God. In your journal, write how you feel about submission. Be honest with the Lord. He already knows. We're just doing this so you can process your feelings.

P.S. Remember to bring your "item" that represents your vanity fast to put in the box this week!

START
FRESH
TODAY!

The **Inner Quality** } A Deeper Look at Yourself

COMPLIMENTS. WE LIKE TO GET THEM.

I remember a few hilarious ones I've heard.

"You look absolutely great, Rachel. When are ya gonna have that baby?" (My dad complimenting my high school cheerleading coach two months after she had the baby!)

"Your brother is so handsome. Is he married?" (My tenth-grade science teacher about my dad!!)

"Your hair looks so much better than it used to." (An elderly woman in my life complimenting me after she thought I was using her hair pudding.)

Psychology Today has issued studies that make a sad statement about compliments. Most of them have to do with personal appearance, performance, and possessions. Sad, isn't it? No one seems to notice what really counts: what's inside of us.

In high school or college I wrote this phrase: "Who I am in private is far more than I am in public." It was my personal reminder that my internal self mattered far more than all the external stuff everyone else saw. I knew my inner heart, and that was the real truth of who I was.

HOW'S YOUR INNER BEAUTY?

It's so easy to get caught up in the latest fads and diets and hairstyles. But God cares about what you're wearing on your heart more than anything else.

This week, we're going to get to the heart of it. We're going to try to get your internal wardrobe to be "all that"!

A lot of times, who we are inside comes out of our mouths when we are with others. Ever been with a beautiful person who becomes less and less beautiful the more you get to know her? Or one who seems just average until you see her stunning beauty come out from inside? What's happening is that you're seeing her inner beauty by what comes out of her mouth.

What's coming out of yours?

LET'S TRY A LITTLE TEST.

1. **When friends decide they want to hang out doing a certain thing you'd rather not do, do you:**
   a. Distance yourself and hold a grudge
   b. Keep talking to try to overpower the majority and get your way
   c. Listen to everyone's feelings and try to bring about a happy compromise

2. **When you've just gotten another long writing assignment from your lit teacher, do you:**
   a. Refuse to do it because she's assigned way too much this quarter
   b. Do it but bad-mouth the teacher to your parents and friends
   c. Do it—she's the teacher and you're called to respect her

3. **When your mom asks you to take out the trash just as you sit down for the first time all day, do you:**
   a. Throw a royal fit
   b. Grumble under your breath and do it . . . grumpily
   c. Do it with all your heart to please your mom

4. **When your little brother wants the same computer you had planned to use to IM your best friend, do you:**

   a. Tease him the whole time while you use it
   b. Tell him what you think he should be doing
   c. Let him go first

5. **When you think someone has made a mistake, do you:**

   a. Want to be the first to correct it
   b. Try to take over because you can lead better
   c. Try to cover it up until you can mention it quietly to the person

6. **Do you go to church because:**

   a. You have to, but you hate it
   b. You have good friends there, and it's a great social outlet
   c. You love God and want to be in His house

OKAY, } SCORE IT.

Were you mostly a's?
You are wearing the wrong stuff, girlfriend!
Were you mostly b's?
You could try harder to wear better stuff inside.
Were you mostly c's?
Great! Keep up the good work!

♥ **LET'S LOOK AT A FEW THINGS GOD REALLY LIKES US TO WEAR INSIDE.**

WHAT DOES SK SAY?

"Check out chapter 6 in *Secret Keeper* for a fresh perspective on Bathsheba."
—Dannah Gresh

DAY 1

Read Esther 4:5–16

{ I delight greatly in the Lord; my soul rejoices in my God. For he has clothed me with garments of salvation and arrayed me in a robe of righteousness.
Isaiah 61:10

OKAY, YOU'RE PROBABLY IN YOUR TEENS, RIGHT? And probably you're protective of your little sisters in Christ. Well, have you noticed that trashy T-shirt messages are being sold to younger and younger girls? Years ago Lexi and I were in a children's store. She brought me a T-shirt that read, "I only go to school to meet boys." For cryin' out loud, the shirt was for little girls! Another one read, "Bad Attitude. Proud of it." And lately I've been seeing more and more T-shirts that boast about horrible sin. I saw some in a store recently that are too vulgar to quote.

It reminds me of what the apostle Paul writes in 1 Corinthians 5:1–2 when he comments that there is a man committing incest with his father's wife. He writes, "And you are proud [of it]!" Times haven't really changed, have they?

Does what YOU wear speak as loudly about who YOU are? Does the care and modesty with which you dress say quietly, "I'm a woman of worth"? Are you quick to make statements of your belief with your attire?

I'm afraid that sometimes we want to be non-offensive, and so we seek this neutral position. That's dangerous thinking. As I was just reading in *Christianity Today*, Chuck Colson wrote, "We are also called to fulfill the cultural commission. Christians are agents of God's saving grace— bringing others to Christ—but we are also agents of his common grace; sustaining and renewing his creation, defending the created institutions of family and society, critiquing false worldviews."

Colson went on to say, "If we're tempted to ignore the great moral issues of our day, or dismiss them as 'just politics,' we are betraying our biblical mandate and our own heritage. Nothing could be deadlier for the church, nor the culture, since real Christianity invariably provides a healthy influence on society." Are you influencing this world for good as loudly as some are influencing it for evil?

Inner wardrobe must-have for all seasons? Boldness for Christ!

♥ **IN YOUR JOURNAL TODAY** . . . In your reading today, you saw that Esther was willing to stand up for her faith even in the face of death. God blessed her and all her people mightily for it. We aren't called to risk death—just sometimes risk losing a little pride. Oh, God forgive us! In your journal can you write about a time when you did not stand up for your faith and confess it? Then write about a time when you did, and thank God for the things that came out of it.

WE ARE
AGENTS OF HIS
**COMMON
GRACE!**

WEEK 6
THE INNER QUALITY
DAY 2

Read Numbers 12:1–3

{ Do not . . . take pride in one man over against another. For who makes you different from anyone else? What do you have that you did not receive? And if you did receive it, why do you boast as though you did not? 1 Corinthians 4:6–7

DID YOU SEE THE ANIMATED FILM *SHARK TALE?* Funny movie. There's one character in there that got me thinking: Sykes. He's the puffer fish who owns the whale wash and obviously has some sly business deals going on. You might say he suffers from panic attacks. When the going gets tough, he's always full of hot air. The character is a riot, but he's based on a real fish.

The puffer fish is also known as the blowfish, fugu, swellfish, and globefish. It is called the puffer fish because when it is threatened, it puffs up to about twice its normal size by gulping water. In this engorged state, the puffer fish can swim at only about half its normal speed. Its defense mechanism actually slows it down!

I think that's a brilliant word picture for pride. Pride puffs us up, but in the end it just slows us down. We can't talk about the internal wardrobe this week without addressing pride. The apostle Paul mentions pride six times in his first letter to the Corinthians. He must have felt they were addicted to pride.

Truth is, so are we sometimes.

I know few solid, world-changing believers who haven't confessed to me that they've battled an ugly war with pride. I certainly have. We're simply puffed up, and it slows us down, keeping us from what we're called to do.

As Paul challenges, "What do you have that you did not receive?" He's talking of spiritual gifts and qualities. That's, sadly, where I see some Christians getting all full of hot air. They think themselves very spiritual. Oh, please—what do we have that we did not receive from God?

Moses certainly had a lot of power and authority from God. So much, that even Miriam and Aaron opposed him.

His own brother and sister got to gossiping and stirring others up. (Sounds like a hall full of girls having PMS, really!) Does Moses fight back? Prove himself? Nope. The next verse is telling. Moses was "more humble than anyone else on the face of the earth" (Numbers 12:3). He wore humility on his heart and never got full of hot air!

Let's all take a little breather from being puffed up, shall we? Maybe then, the church will be able to swim a little faster through the chaos and sin of our culture!

Fashion forecast for your future: Humility.

♥ **IN YOUR JOURNAL TODAY** ... Are you a puffer fish? Do you tend to be filled with pride? How can you know? I think that truth-telling is a good barometer. Not truth-telling about others. (That's gossip!) Are you willing to be truthful about your own weaknesses, mistakes, dreams, and hopes? If that makes you a little uncomfortable, maybe you should ask for a greater dose of humility. Tell a few truths right now.

ASK
FOR A
GREATER
DOSE OF
HUMILITY.

WEEK 6
THE INNER QUALITY

DAY 3

Read Genesis 4:2–16

{ "Why are you angry? Why is your face down-cast? If you do what is right, will you not be accepted? But if you do not do what is right, sin is crouching at your door; it desires to have you, but you must master it." Genesis 4:6–7

GOD'S WORD TELLS US A CHRISTIAN SHOULD BE JOYFUL.
Joy is a garment we wear as evidence that our lives have power over the evil in this world. So what happens when a Christian gets depressed? I know. I've been there.

Three years ago, after a terribly painful situation in my life, I became confused and slow of judgment; I slurred my speech and mixed up words. Though it was funny for me to look at my kids and say, "Bring the bunny" when I really meant the goldfish they'd just won at the fair, it was also somewhat concerning. I finally admitted I was depressed and needed medication and planned to go see a doctor the next day. A six-month course of antidepressants had helped me one other time years before.

My mom encouraged me first to pray to ask God if the depression was physical or spiritual. I did. In a few days, the root issue of my own sin and hurt had been discovered. In one single prayer session at two o'clock in the morning, I felt the healing come forth. I moved forward, drug-free and healthy.

More and more I meet teenage girls who are on anti-depressants. I'm open to the idea of using medication to heal the brain, but I think sometimes we turn to it too quickly. It's really important to first see if there is a spiritual issue at hand.

God gives us a recipe for depression in Genesis 4. We see Cain suffering from depression because his fruit wasn't as acceptable to God as Abel's animal sacrifice. The fact is, Cain had missed the mark of God's best. He'd sinned. God called for an animal sacrifice, not something fruity! In Cain's depression, God comes and says to him, "If you do what is right, will you not be accepted?" If Cain could stop sinning and start living right, he'd return to his joy.

Sometimes sadness is a result of loss or someone's sin against us, but sometimes depression is God allowing us to feel the disconnection from Him created by our own sin. The next time you struggle with sadness or depression, first ask God, "Is there anything in my life that is displeasing to You?"

What's every girl of God seen wearing? Joyfulness!

♥ **IN YOUR JOURNAL TODAY** . . . Examine your own mental health today. Are you happy? Sad? Depressed? Write down a summary of your feelings. Then, if there is any sadness or depression, ask God if there is any sin He wants you to deal with. Spend time writing in your journal about anything He helps you to see. Then seek out your mom or youth leader to pray with you through the issue, expecting God to restore your joy as you obey Him and stop sinning.

GOD
SAYS A
CHRISTIAN
SHOULD BE
JOYFUL!

{ I also want women to dress . . . not with braided hair or gold or pearls or expensive clothes, but with good deeds, appropriate for women who profess to worship God. 1 Timothy 2:9–10

GOOD DEEDS. They're the must-have accessory for every woman who worships God.

I teach high school health at Grace Prep, a Christian high school. I love it. We spend one whole quarter studying psychology and preparing for the event of the quarter: Random Acts of Kindness. The mission: Each student must randomly deliver good will to people they do not know. During his freshman year, my son joined with a few other guys to deliver fresh-baked cookies to people in the neighborhood surrounding the school. You can imagine what people thought of high school boys delivering fresh baked goods. They wondered what was baked into them. They were suspicious. They made jokes. They laughed. They accused them of intending to ask for a donation. People could hardly accept the good deeds.

The story of one woman and her daughter certainly proved it was worth it. She wrote my son a letter a few weeks later. She said thank you and apologized for making fun of their little box of cookies and saying it might have a dead rat in it. Then she explained how that little box had changed their lives, if only a little bit. You see, her husband had died not long before that, and she and her daughter were feeling really lonely, really hopeless. She was beginning to ask if God really cared. The fact that some freshman high school boys would care enough to bake up some cookies and deliver them was, to her, a very big message from God. He did, indeed, still care.

When was the last time you showed God's love in a practical way? Maybe babysit for free for the single mom next door. It'll blow her away when you simply say, "I can't accept payment. This is a random act of kindness to show

God's love in a practical way." You could wash the windows on the pet tanks for your biology teacher one day. Just take your bottle of Windex and paper towels and show up armed. Tell your teacher, "I'd like to wash your pet tanks as a random act of kindness to show God's love in a practical way." Blow her away! Perhaps you could just buy a bundle of daffodils on a cold, winter day and stand on the corner and hand them out. Or you could go visit an elderly woman who doesn't have anyone to talk to. Read her your favorite book.

A woman who worships God naturally does good deeds.

Abigail's good deed to David and his men saved her life . . . and the lives of her servants. I'm not asking you to stop a war— just to stop some sadness!

{ ♥ IN YOUR JOURNAL TODAY . . .
You have no directed journal entry today.

Go out and commit a random act of KINDNESS!

{ I have stilled and quieted my soul; like a weaned child with its mother, like a weaned child is my soul within me. Psalm 131:2

A FEW YEARS AGO I WENT THROUGH A VERY PAINFUL TIME. I was rejected by some of the people I had trusted all my life long. During that time, I cried nearly every day. I drew closer and closer to God for comfort and often asked Him, "Don't You see my pain? Why don't You stop it if You see it?"

We have times like that, when God allows us to hurt though He'd rather not. Do you know what I mean? Why does God allow this? Because He wants us to wear every good inner fashion, including contentment.

During my summer of pain, I kept seeing some crazy words in my head. They looked like "L-h Roi" and I knew to say it "la ha roy!" When I entered into deep prayer time with God, sometimes I'd repeat these words over and over again as a prayer. I didn't exactly know why, but I knew they comforted me greatly. Again and again they slipped from my tongue and from my spirit.

Months later, I was reading Genesis 16. Poor Hagar had only done what her mistress had asked when she had sex with Abraham to produce an heir. We don't know anything about how she felt. She may have truly hated that act and been ashamed of it. The fact that later on she is accused of despising Sarah alludes to the fact that she may have been a reluctant rather than eager participant. (I mean, Abraham was already very old!)

Finally, Hagar runs away from Sarah and finds herself in that place of isolation and rejection. She probably wondered, "God, do You see my pain?" He did. He came to her and comforted her—not by changing things but simply by being with her. And she named the place, Beer Lahai Roi, which means, "Well of the Living One who sees me."

I nearly had a heart attack. Those were my words! Had I read them years ago and subconsciously remembered them? Had God supernaturally given them to me? I don't know. I don't care. I only know that when I spoke them, He was there. He didn't change my situation. But I was comforted simply by His presence.

That's what Psalm 131 speaks of—being in the presence of God without clamoring like a baby for milk.

A woman of God learns to be content. Her soul is still and quiet, even in hard times.

Is yours?

♥ IN YOUR JOURNAL TODAY . . . Write about a time when you really felt God's presence. You KNEW He was watching. He sees you. Celebrate that!

BE
CONTENT.

7

The Bottom Line } A Love Story

Z.

That's not a typo. It's how my sweetheart signs his love notes to me. His name is Bob, but I call him Z or Zeener. It's a sick and twisted story, to be honest. But when we first got married we called each other "Sweetheart." After a while, this digressed to a lesser but more affectionate "Sweet-ert," which became "Ert-wa," which became "Ertwa-zeenie," which became "Zeenfelder," which became "Zeenie" and has settled at "Zeener," which is often just shortened to "Z" when we write love notes. I know these sound almost, or perhaps entirely, childish, but to me they are so beautiful. They are our love names for each other.

In fact, I feel a bit foolish sharing them. They're not yours to use; they are mine and his alone, and they mean nothing to anyone outside of our love.

God has a never-before-uttered love name just for you. Did you know that Jesus has a lover's name that He'll one day give to you? In Revelation 2:17 He says, "To him who overcomes, I will give some of the hidden manna. I will also give him a white stone with a new name written on it, known only to him who receives it."

Even before a little bit of research, I wrote in my Bible, "My love name from God" beside this verse. It's so thrilling for me to think that He has one of these precious white stones just for me with a special name I've never heard uttered.

Of course, I'm a nut for researching biblical meanings, and so I did. It seems the Greeks and Romans were accustomed to using white stones and black stones for people on trial. When the verdict was to be read, rather than speaking they slipped a black stone to a person who was guilty. If they slipped them a white stone, it meant they were innocent, justified, acquitted, and victorious! Bible scholars agree that the white stone definitely signifies God's personal announcement of each believer's acquittal. This thrills my heart.

As for the name, there are two widely held beliefs. One coincides with my first impression—that God has a never-before-uttered love name just for me and just for you that He's written on our individual stones. This completes the portrait of His adopting us into His family. You see, it's our "new name." Our love relationship will become fully active.

The other belief is that this name is one for Jesus Christ, which has never been heard. It's a protected name. No man has ever blasphemed this precious name. Only those of us who spend eternity with Jesus because we've accepted His free gift of salvation will know it. It is spotless.

Either way, it's a love name. Mine or His. Yours or His.

Let's focus on the thought of an intimate love relationship with Jesus this week. I truly believe this is our only true and foolproof motivation for living a modest, pure, and virtuous life.

💜 **EACH DAY I WANT TO ASK YOU THE SAME QUESTION:**
DO YOU LOVE HIM?

"Check out God's love letter to you on page 85 of *Secret Keeper.*"
—Dannah Gresh

DAY 1

Read John 14:15–21

{ "Whoever has my commands and obeys them, he is the one who loves me. He who loves me will be loved by my Father, and I too will love him and show myself to him." John 14:21

AS YOU ALREADY KNOW, MY FAMILY HAS ENJOYED AN AFRICAN SAFARI. As you enter the safari land, there are signs that say again and again that under no circumstances should you exit your vehicle. These animals are wild, after all. As my family entered the park, we soon discovered we were all alone for miles and miles on dirt roads as we sought our ranger site. In our haste to arrive, we went over a bump a little too fast, knocked a hole in our oil pan, and seized the engine. That meant we weren't going anywhere ever again in that vehicle.

In the middle of nowhere, as the African heat began to get the best of us, we sat for what seemed like hours— though it was really only about one hour. Occasionally, Bob was tempted to start walking to see what help he could find. There seemed to be a ranger station not far from where we were. Instead we prayed. I remember it well. "Lord, we know You need us to obey this rule to stay in the car, but sitting here in the heat seems dangerous as well. Can You please send help?" Soon after, a man drove by. He was going to our exact destination and offered us a ride.

The next day we found out two chilling things. The morning we were stuck, a male lion had been spotted by the rangers on that very road. He was hungry and looking for prey. A week earlier, two tourists had spotted a male lion resting and decided to get out for a better view. It ate one of them.

It pays to obey.

Remember when I called Satan a roaring lion seeking to devour you? Well, your Father wants to protect you. How? By vigilantly watching for the presence of the Enemy and calling to you when you're about to run across a trap. God doesn't want us to obey out of fear, though. He wants us to obey out of our great love for Him. He tells us in John 14 that the proof of our love is in obedience.

Do you love Him?

{ ♥ **IN YOUR JOURNAL TODAY** . . . Today in your journal I want you to consider, do you love Him? But I have a specific way I want you to do this. Look back over the last twenty-four hours. Did you obey your parents? (He commands that!) Did you spend time in His Word and in prayer? (We are told to pray without ceasing.) Did you obey your teachers by handing in work on time? (We are instructed to study to show ourselves approved.)

IT PAYS TO
OBEY.

DAY 2

Read Exodus 31:1–3, 37:1–10

{ Your body is a temple of the Holy Spirit, who is in you, whom you have received from God . . . You are not your own; you were bought at a price. Therefore honor God with your body. 1 Corinthians 6:19–20

IT'S THE MOST EXPENSIVE PIECE OF FURNITURE EVER SOLD. The Badminton Cabinet was commissioned by a British duke, who was not even nineteen years old, to be created in Florence, Italy, by the Foggini family. Both the duke who helped design it and the family who crafted it are credited with ingenious taste. The piece is applauded for combining architecture, sculpting, and painting, and for utilizing lapis lazuli, agate, Sicilian red and green jasper, as well as chalcedony, amethyst quartz, and other superb hard stones. It sold for $36 million in 2004.

Just imagine what the value of the ark of the covenant would be if ever we discovered its sequestered and protected location. God was the commissioner. He had very clear guidelines as to how it would be created. Bezalel was the craftsman. I once thought the items in the temple must have been crudely made, but notice Exodus 31:3. The Holy Spirit gave him a special spiritual gift of craftsmanship. Wow! Talk about some amazing pieces of art.

You, too, are a carefully commissioned and crafted work of art. But the commissioner, God, is also your craftsman. What value there is in you! First Corinthians tells us that your value is so great that the Holy Spirit chooses to dwell within you when invited. What a masterpiece you are! Worth far more than any $36 million cabinet—and even more than the ark, should it happen to be found.

What makes you so valuable is not just the fact that God made you, but that Christ purchased you just like that Badminton Cabinet was purchased at an auction in

2004. At just about the year AD 33 Jesus bought you with His blood. What greater value is there than the life of our Savior? No value can be placed upon it.

This is your motivation to love and obey Him: that you have been crafted and purchased.

You are His masterpiece.

♥ **IN YOUR JOURNAL TODAY** . . . You are a masterpiece, crafted and commissioned and bought at the highest possible price. How does that make you feel? Do you believe it? I know this world makes it hard to receive that truth, so if you're hurting or feeling unlovely, pour it out to God. I pray that you are beginning to sense your beauty as you soak yourself in God's presence, deep under the surface of society. If so, then praise Him. Oh, how I'd love to hear that you've written a sonnet of praise to Him today. Let's write a Psalm 151, a psalm of praise about you—one of His master creations. It's not bragging; it's boasting in Him. Even if you don't believe it, write it. His truth will come.

WHAT
VALUE
THERE IS
IN YOU!

WEEK 7
THE BOTTOM LINE

DAY 3

{ I also want women to dress modestly. 1 Timothy 2:9

Read Genesis 39:1–12

IMAGINE BEING JOSEPH. You've just been plopped into the business of one of the wealthiest guys in the world and his beautiful wife is a babe—and she digs you. But wait—we can't understand this temptation unless we bring it to modern day.

Place yourself in Hollywood, you're working for an agent who works with Ashton Kutcher. And he digs you! Sure, he's hot for Demi Moore, but he'd also like to get a little action with you. Oh, he doesn't say so. He comes close, makes your heart beat wild with desire, and whispers in your ear, "You are the most beautiful woman I've ever known. I can't help myself."

What do you do?

Melt?

Or run?

Joseph ran. That was God's command, and Joseph did what was right in God's eyes.

His obedience should be a grand inspiration to us. As my mom used to say, "no ifs, ands, or buts." Just straight-out obedience.

NOW, TURN THE TABLES.

Imagine that Ashton Kutcher is a man after God's own heart. (Oh, I wish. Maybe you could pray for him today. Imagine if all of the Secret Keepers who read this prayed for him to come to know our Savior.) Anyway, imagine he loves God. He's gorgeous. And you . . . well, you are a woman like Potiphar's wife. You throw on a pair of very low, low-riders, a nice tight baby pink T that's cropped to show off your toned and tanned stomach complete with belly button ring. And your hair just playfully brushes the skin of your lower back when you turn around.

Are you acting like Joseph, obeying without question? Or are you Potiphar's wife, tempting and seducing with how you dress?

God only addresses modesty four times in the Bible. (My mom always said it was only obedience if she only had to tell me once!) The clearest directive is in 1 Timothy: "I also want women to dress modestly."

Do you dress modestly? Do you obey Him?

Or should I ask . . . do you love Him?

♥ **IN YOUR JOURNAL TODAY** . . . Sit quietly in God's presence, and ask Him to reveal to you any outfits that are immodest. Is there a tiny T that's cropped too high? A tight shirt or sweater? Let me put it this way: It's okay to feel good and even beautiful when you've finished dressing. But is there something you wear that makes you feel sexy? That's a good sign that it should go. Can you obey God today by trashing the outfits He brings to mind? Do you love Him?

OBEY
WITHOUT
QUESTION!

WEEK 7
THE BOTTOM LINE

DAY 4

{ Do not merely listen to the word, and so deceive yourselves. Do what it says. James 1:22

Read Numbers 22:21–31

STORMIE—SHE'S OUR LABRADOODLE. After Robby and Lexi begged for nearly three years, I reluctantly gave in to the family pleas for a puppy—under one condition. She had to live in the basement.

No exceptions.

Bob and I picked her up at the Philadelphia airport on December 22nd. Only five pounds and hiding under anything she could find, she was adorable. I remember holding her up to look into her eyes, but she just pouted and tried not to look at me.

I loved her instantly. She slept in my lap the whole way home. Five minutes after arriving, she was snuggled tightly into my bed.

On the second floor of our home. As in, two floors from the basement. She never really spends a lot of time in the basement. I love her far too much to remove her from my presence—and my blessing.

There are some things I don't let Stormie do, though. She cannot chew on rocks, though she craves them. She could choke. (I've looked and looked for an alternative, and she loves ice cubes.) She cannot run out of my yard. We have a rather busy road just behind our property, and I don't want her to get hit by a car. (But I've modified my life and have begun walking so she can enjoy the thrill of exploring.) I love her, so I'm teaching her to obey me.

Do you see where I am going?

God asks us to obey out of love. And when we don't, He will do what He must to get our attention. Nothing tells that truth so well as Balaam's donkey. Can you believe that God actually made that thing talk?!

Balaam was a man who'd heard God's Word but didn't do what He said. We can be like that. We hear God wants us to dress modestly or wait for marriage for intimacy or save ourselves emotionally for just one man, but doing it is so hard. It can seem like no one else is waiting! But everyone else isn't whom God is speaking to right now. He's speaking to you.

No more excuses.

Do you love Him?

Do what He says.

♥ **IN YOUR JOURNAL TODAY** . . . Do you have a pet you love? One that just wraps your heart around its paw? If so, write about your love for it. Maybe it's a hamster that grabs the rungs of the cage and peers out at you, and you just have to get it out to squeeze it. Maybe it's a snotty cat that whisks his tail teasingly at you, and you never stop reaching for it. If not a pet, how about a younger sibling, cousin, or tot who softens your heart? Write about how love for him or her can help you understand God's love for you.

OBEY
OUT OF
LOVE!

WEEK 7
THE BOTTOM LINE

DAY 5

Read 1 Samuel 1:21–28

{ Ask and it will be given to you; seek and you will find; knock and the door will be opened to you. For everyone who asks receives; he who seeks finds; and to him who knocks, the door will be opened. Matthew 7:7–8

AS I'VE BEEN WRITING THIS BOOK, STORMIE KEEPS ASKING ME TO PLAY. I can't say no. It's impossible. When she looks at me with those adoring eyes and squeaks her toy with her mouth all awkwardly wrapped around it, I have only two choices: I can kiss her nose, or I can play with her.

As a result, the time I had to write this afternoon turned into playtime for Stormie. So it's evening—10:46 p.m., to be exact—and I'm still writing.

About twenty minutes ago, she came back. This time she just sat in front of me longingly. Each time I looked away she barked, and when I turned toward her she gave me that half-cocked puppy head with eyes I could not resist.

"No, Stormie," I'd say. "I cannot play."

Woof! Woof! Woof! was her reply.

So I found my family. I begged them to play with her.

"Unless you play with her," I explained, "I simply cannot write. I have to know she's being played with."

I delight in giving this new love of my life what she asks for. Mind you, she's not spoiled. (Okay, maybe a little.) We're disciplining her, crate-training her, potty training her—and I'm loving her more than I'd imagined I could.

If we, who are mere humans, cannot help but give lavishly to our puppies, how much more does the Father desire to give us good things! He gave Hannah a baby. He's given me so many desires of my heart I cannot count them all.

At its heart, immodesty is manipulation. It's failing to trust in God to supply attention and perhaps even the love of our earthly life.

Let's put that to an end—no more manipulation. Just ask the Father. Every good and perfect gift you will ever have comes from Him.

And now, if you don't mind, I will go find Stormie.
It's time to play.

♥ IN YOUR JOURNAL TODAY ...

Ask God to fulfill your desires. What is the one thing you
want most from Him? To have your parents stay together?
To find a godly husband—one day? To live closer to your dad?
Go ahead. Ask. He absolutely delights in answering you.
Oh, and if He doesn't answer at first, take a tip from Stormie.
She keeps asking. So should we. It builds our faith, and that's
the biggest gift He'll ever give to you.

TIME TO
PLAY!

WELCOME TO THE
THIRTY-FIVE DAY PLUNGE.

This *Secret Keeper* Power Pak is designed so a reader can pick it up and go to a deeper level of intimacy with God on her own, but it's best used as a group experience.

Teaching modesty has become a more and more difficult task. Our culture has become so immune to the sensuality, that we now see little girls pressured to dress like sexy grown women. Thongs are the norm, not the exception. Low cut shirts are commonplace. Moms often set bad examples for the teens you're trying to influence.

Our job lies before us. We need to convince the girls we love that being able to breathe in a shirt is a good thing! Let's impassion them to discern what's right and what's wrong, what's modest and what will give them away to be trashed.

HOW?

By having fun! Shouldn't fashion be fun? I think so. So don't expect this Bible study to feel like homework. No way! Instead, prepare to plunge into fun. (Think: facials, fashion shows, shopping challenges, and great girl talk!)

WHAT ARE WE WAITING FOR?
LET'S DIVE IN!

PLUNGE 1 } GO DEEP

FOR YOUR FIRST WEEK, you'll be handing out the Power Paks and getting the girls pumped up.

What do you need? Water! Lots of water!

You could have a pool party or a water balloon fight. You could head to the beach or a water park. Just get them wet!

LEADER'S PREPARATION

- Review the "Go Deep" introductory reading for week one on pages 7–12.

- Collect bottled water for each girl with made-by-you labels that read "Go Deep!"

- Plan some water fun (pool party, beach day, water balloon fight, water slides).

THE ACTUAL PLUNGE

Start with fun! Water wars, swimming, etc. Just let the girls have fun—and join in! (A great game I just love is to cover a watermelon with Crisco and plop it into a pool. Play watermelon "football" in the water with the slippery watermelon. It's a blast!)

After they've had a chance to dry off, give each gal a bottle of water and a Secret Keeper Power Pak. Explain your passion in doing this particular study with them. Then just let them read the introductory "Go Deep" text beginning on page 7 while they enjoy their bottled water.

♥ **GIRL GAB!** } Break into small groups and let the girls talk about going deep. Ask them if they've ever felt like they're stuck at the surface of Christianity, not really experiencing the power God promises in His Word. Maybe let some of them share stories of when they really encountered God to fuel the desire to go deep. Invite them to watch for moments this week when the waves of life seem to be crashing against them, and encourage them to simply dive into God's presence right then and there with a quick prayer.

OPTIONAL INCENTIVE

For the next six weeks, these girls need to commit to do their devos five out of every seven days. Their experience won't be nearly as powerful if they don't participate in the at-home devos. Offer an incentive. A shopping spree. A sleepover. Anything. It's okay to reward them for getting into the Word of God! Once they see the spiritual and emotional rewards, they won't need tangible rewards, but we've got to get them there first.

PLUNGE 2 } THE EVOLUTION

THE GOAL THIS WEEK is just to warm up the girls' hearts and get them talking about how ridiculous fashion can be.

What do you need? Really foolish examples of things you used to wear. (I would probably pull out my Guess overalls from 1985. I might even wear them with a pair of white sneakers and doubled up colored socks to tuck the jeans into. Still can't believe we did that!) If you don't have anything you used to wear, hit up a friend or a vintage store to borrow some comedic fashion.

LEADER'S PREPARATION

● Review the "Evolution" reading for week two on page 35.

● Collect some fashion magazines.

● Bring your old clothes or find some vintage options.

THE ACTUAL PLUNGE

Model your old clothes or bring them out for the girls to laugh a little. If you can find some pictures of you in them (with your funky hair or silly makeup—once thought to be so cool), bring them too. The goal is to laugh a little and open a dialogue about how foolish fashion can be.

Have one of the girls read Proverbs 7:6–27 out loud. Then contrast it by having another girl read Proverbs 31:10–31 out loud. Take a moment to talk about specifically how fashion has played a role in your ability to live in either or both of these "definitions." (I would probably talk about a time when I very stupidly chose to wear something terribly immodest to a company party. It was classic Proverbs 7 behavior. Then I might share a time when I said no to a really cute sundress because it was a little short. That was a Proverbs 31 moment.)

♥ GIRL GAB! } Break into small groups and let the girls talk about whether what they wear tends to be more Proverbs 7 or more Proverbs 31 kind of clothing. Ask them to be really honest about considering which one they are and which one they want to be: a Proverbs 7 or 31 woman.

PLUNGE 3 } TRUTH OR BARE FASHION TESTS!

FOR THIS WEEKLY PLUNGE, YOU'LL BE HOSTING A FABULOUS FASHION SHOW, complete with snacks and hors d'oeuvres! Go crazy with atmosphere. Get spotlights, strobe lights, mirror balls, a bubble machine, or a red carpet! (These are often rented for $10–$20.) Throw down rose petals, confetti, or large glitter pieces where the girls will be walking. If you know a hip hair stylist and makeup artist who would be willing to donate time to your youth group, ask them to come and tastefully glam up the girls. You will be looking at and talking about current fashion trends and running the *Secret Keeper* Truth or Bare Fashion Tests on them.

LEADER'S PREPARATION

● BEFORE you collect the items needed below, review the Truth or Bare Fashion Tests found in chapter 3 of the updated *Secret Keeper*. The clothes you select for your fashion show must be able to pass the fashion tests.

ITEMS NEEDED:

● Decorations for fashion show (strobe light, mirror ball, confetti, etc.)

● Hors d'oeuvres or snacks

● Upbeat Christian music CD (something with a great beat for the "runway")

● Index cards (for your MC to read clothing descriptions)

● Lots of fashionable clothes!

The fashion show outfits should be of varying sizes and styles. For example, you might put together a "cowgirl" look in a size 0 and a funky "hippie" look in a size 11. If you have the budget, buy the clothes, which you could give to each girl after modeling. Or approach a local store that might be willing to loan you clothes in exchange for mentioning their name. As a last resort, ask for donations for the evening with the understanding the clothes will be returned after this session. If your group is small, you may try to have an outfit for each girl. If you have a large group, you can just have 4–7 great showstoppers. Here are a few ideas for clothing that hit problem areas effectively:

- An adorable sweat suit WITHOUT words across the fanny!
- A pair of low-riders with our "secret weapon"—a long T-shirt (Go ahead and put a short T on top for a trendy look!)
- Some cool, trendy shorts with a 5" or 7" inseam
- A peasant top or sheer top WITH a T-shirt or tank top under it

PREPARATION

You will need to write up index cards with a description of each outfit you come up with. When doing this, try to get into "runway fashion show" mode and have fun with the descriptions! The card should include a rundown of the look you're going for and how it combats certain modesty issues. Here's a sample:

"First we have (name of girl) with a great example of how a girl can modestly wear low-rider pants. These pants have a denim look with a brushed cotton feel. How does she get this great look without compromise? That's our 'secret weapon!' What's a secret weapon? It's a tank top with a nice loooong torso so it can be tucked into the low riders. You may find these in trendy colors in some department stores, but for a sure bet grab a few whities in the men's department! This way you still get the low-rider look without being immodest. These pants actually came with that funky belt, for those of you who are accessory impaired. Oh, the versatility!"

THE ACTUAL PLUNGE

Invite the girls to enjoy hors d'oeuvres and find a place near the runway. You will have preselected several models or you can select them as the girls socialize.

After you present some challenging thoughts about modesty from chapter 1 of *Secret Keeper*, you must let them see what modesty actually looks like. Have the MC get the audience all pumped up and in the right frame of mind to have a blast and clap and cheer. Play the music and have the models come down the aisle one at a time as the MC reads the index card about each particular outfit. Encourage the models to have fun with spins and turns.

Finally, it's time for the Truth or Bare Fashion Tests. Have the models fall into line on the stage. Have fun explaining each test. (Go ahead and laugh. Who can talk about "breasts" without a good giggle?) Have each of the models do the tests on themselves before the audience, taking time to discuss possible remedies if an outfit fails one of the tests. For some of the tests, you can even have the audience participate.

♥ GIRL GAB! } **Break into small groups and let the girls talk about the fashion show. Which outfits did they like? Which ones didn't they like as much? Go over the Truth or Bare Fashion Tests and let the girls push each other, asking them what tests their wardrobe might consistently fail. Have a time of prayer, allowing the girls time to bring their thoughts before God.**

PLUNGE 4 } A FATHER'S THOUGHTS!

IT'S TIME TO BRING A GUY'S BRAIN TO THE TABLE! Look around your church and find three or four really cool dads. These need to be dads who have a good relationship with their daughters—maybe not perfect but good. They need to be dads who have a solid relationship with Jesus. And finally, they need to be willing to talk about the way a guy thinks when he sees girls dressed immodestly.

LEADER'S PREPARATION

- Review the "A Father's Thoughts" introduction found on pages 67–68.

- Collect basketballs, volleyballs, or other equipment to play some ball with the dads.

- Select your panel of dads. Ask one to prepare a special devotion from a dad's heart on his desire for these girls to be virtuous. Many of the girls will have dads who either are not concerned about modesty and purity or who are not comfortable addressing those subjects with their daughters. This may be the only father/daughter talk on purity some of them ever get. Let it come from his heart. He may share a real-life story or some of what he's heard guys say about immodest girls. Make sure he selects a special Bible verse to share. A simple ten-minute challenge will do. The other dads will participate in Q&A with the girls. Encourage them to prepare to answer questions about how a guy thinks and why modesty matters.

THE ACTUAL PLUNGE

Start this plunge officially with some dads vs. daughters physical challenges such as a game of volleyball or basketball or even just good old-fashioned dodge ball!

After everyone has worked up a good sweat, introduce the dad who will be giving the devotional from a father's heart. Let him loose!

♥ **GIRL GAB!** } **Girl Gab tonight is a Q&A session. Let the girls ask the dads questions you've collected about how a guy thinks. These are some good starter questions if the girls need some help:**

- When you were younger, wasn't it the girls who dressed trendy that attracted you?

- If so, why would I want to dress modestly?

- Don't guys like it when girls are sexy?

- How do I get a guy to be romantic?

- When is the right time to get serious about guys?

- Is it okay to wear miniskirts?

- What happens in a guy's mind when a girl wears belly rings?

- Why do guys have such a hard time expressing themselves?

PLUNGE 5 } SLOW DOWN THE FAST WAY!

FOR THIS WEEKLY PLUNGE, YOU'RE GOING TO CALL THE GIRLS TO GO JUST A TAD DEEPER—to distance themselves from this world's appetites with a vanity fast. Before explaining the fast, you'll want to pamper them a bit with a delightful facial. (Yes, you can get in on the action yourself!)

LEADER'S PREPARATION

- Review the "Vanity Fast" introduction found on pages 85–87.

- Secure your facial materials or schedule your facial expert.

- Decorate with candles for a spa-like atmosphere.

- Prepare some cucumber water by slicing a few cukes and put them in pitchers of water; it's a popular spa antioxidant.

- Find a large and very special box, Plexiglas for transparency, if possible.

- Bring an item to symbolize what it is you will be fasting from.

THE ACTUAL PLUNGE

Start this plunge with interacting during the fun of facials. After everyone is sufficiently cleansed and enjoying their cucumber water, it's time to take the girls a little deeper. Invite them to spend some time quietly reading the "Vanity Fast" text beginning on page 86. After they've read it, share with them what is on your own heart as far as to the practices you need to fast from in the days ahead. Place something you've chosen as a symbol into the large box. It's great if it can be Plexiglas so the girls can see what is collected. Tell them you'd like them to add something to the box next week to symbolize something they will fast from until the end of this study. This might include no fashion mags for the rest of the month, or not watching a certain TV show for the rest of the month. They may choose not to spend money on anything fashionable or vain for the month. Or they could just decide to do no makeup for a month. Anything that God puts on their hearts is okay.

If the girls choose a fashion fast, in which they plan to wear only jeans and T's, do encourage them to be obedient and respectful of their parents if they have a wedding to attend or if their parents have a dress code for church. There are perfectly reasonable exceptions. You can talk them through these.

♥ GIRL GAB! } **Break into small groups and let the girls talk about what most influences their fashion and beauty decisions for the worse. Is it magazines? Movies? Television shows? Peers? Ask them to prayerfully consider what they would be willing to fast from for the rest of this study in order to move more deeply into God's truth. Invite them to bring something next week to place in the box to symbolize their fast.**

PLUNGE 6 } LOVE FEAST

FOR THIS WEEKLY PLUNGE, YOU'LL BE HELPING THE GIRLS "FEAST" ON TRUTH ABOUT THEMSELVES. Each girl will receive four special words of encouragement about her beauty. Two of these encouragements will be about external beauty, and two will be about internal beauty.

LEADER'S PREPARATION

- Review the "A Deeper Look at Yourself" introduction found on page 103.

- Secure a fire site or fireplace and campfire materials.

- Collect fixings for s'mores (graham crackers, marshmallows, chocolate, roasting sticks).

- Bring your large, special box to put the vanity fast symbolic items in.

THE ACTUAL PLUNGE

Start this plunge with some yummy s'mores. After all, we're not fasting from food! Then have each girl explain and add her item that represents her fast to the special box. You may want to include a prayer that God would help the girls with this fast and take each one deeper into His heart.

Now it's time to encourage each other with what my friend Erin likes to call a "Love Feast." If you have a very large group of girls, break them into several smaller groups of four to six. Otherwise, stick with the whole group. Explain that the real "food" of the evening is encouragement about beauty, but not just the obvious external beauty. We're talking deep, inner beauty as well. Invite the girls to turn their attention to one girl at a time. Anyone in the group can share one special beauty truth about her with as much detail as she can. The catch is that there must be two beauty truths about her external beauty (for example, "You have the greatest hair. I remember the first time I met you, you had your hair just piled on top of your head to work out, but I could tell even then you had beautiful, long, full locks of golden hair. I have to try not to be envious!"), and two beauty truths about her internal beauty (for example, "I don't know anyone quite as prayerful as you. You just have this reputation for prayer, and it makes you so beautiful. Everyone knows that if she's struggling with something, you're already praying for her. And it seems like you have a direct line with God. I think that's beautiful!"). Go around the group until every girl—including you—has enjoyed a feast of encouragement.

♥ **GIRL GAB!** } **The Love Feast activity will take some time and will include your Girl Gab time for this week.**

PLUNGE 7 } DO YOU LOVE HIM?

IT'S THE LAST WEEK OF TEACHING, and I want you to leave the girls with something tangible to let them know that Jesus loves them and to remind them that our love is expressed through obedience to Him in all areas of life, including modesty. You'll be preparing a special white stone for each girl and presenting it to her during the session.

LEADER'S PREPARATION

- Review the "A Love Story" introductory reading for week 7 on pages 121–122.

- Purchase white stones, one for each girl in the group, at garden supply stores or craft stores that sell large pebbles. You should be able to find white stones, but if you cannot, please paint them so they will fit with the teaching. These should be large enough for you to write on. You'll write on each in colorful tones the name of the girl you'll give it to. Around the edge in smaller letters you'll write, "Do You Love Him?"

THE ACTUAL PLUNGE

Tonight is going to be a night of prayer and dedication to a life of loving Christ—nothing fancy, just biblical ministry. Start the night by inviting each girl to read the "A Love Story" intro on pages 121–122.

Then present their rocks in a way that says that they are special. Perhaps there is a certain song you'd like to put in the CD player for the girls to listen to. Ask them to imagine what might be on the other side of the rock—their love name from or for Jesus. Remember, either way it's a love name.

Instruct them that this rock is for them to place in their rooms as a reminder to love Him at any cost.

❤ **GIRL GAB! }** Spend tonight in deep ministry over each and every girl. If you have many girls, break them into groups of four to six and have one adult leader for each group. Lead the prayer ministry. If you've never done anything like this, let me give you some ideas. Don't just say one two-minute prayer over each girl. Sit quietly and listen for the Holy Spirit's prompting. Any girl in the room may feel it, and when she does, she should pray for her friend. For example, one girl may sense that a Bible verse she read earlier that day is for the one being prayed over. She should reach for her Bible, read it, and then pray the truth of that verse over her, washing her in the Word of God. Another might suddenly feel led to pray for this girl's family and should do so. After more silence, someone could even see a picture of something. For example, someone gets an image of a girl studying—so that person would just pray for her school responsibilities. Sometimes the Spirit gives us little hints of how to pray and we don't entirely get it, but we should pray to that end. Spend as long as it takes over each girl just ministering in prayer. There may be tears or laughter. The group may jump in with boldness or may be somewhat shy. But I do promise it will be uniting and powerful.

OPTIONAL INCENTIVE

This is your last planned night of activity. But perhaps you opted to give the girls an incentive such as a shopping spree or an ice cream sundae party when you were all done with *Secret Keeper Devotions*. In this case, you'll have a celebration gathering one week from now. Have some ice cream for me! My favorite is mint chocolate chip!

NOTES

1. Robert Heath, David Brandt, and Agnes Nairn, "Brand Relationships: Strengthened by Emotion, Weakened by Attention," *Journal of Advertising*, vol. 46, no. 4 (December 2006), 410-419.

2. Elisabeth Elliot, *Let Me Be a Woman* (Carol Stream, IL: Tyndale House), 1999.

3. Anthony Breznican, "Pretty, Tough Women," *USA Today* online, www.usatoday.com/life/movies/news.

4. Dannah Gresh, *What Are You Waiting For?: The One Thing No One Ever Tells You About Sex* (Colorado Springs: Waterbrook Press, 2011), 57.

5. Ravi Zacharias delivered these thoughts at a presentation on Penn State University campus in March of 2005.

SECRET KEEPER

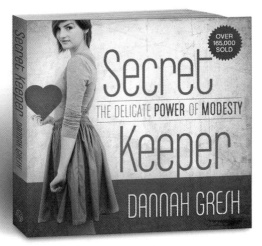

OVER 165,000 SOLD

Secret Keeper
THE DELICATE POWER OF MODESTY
DANNAH GRESH

978-0-8024-3977-2

for other books, blog, events by Dannah Gresh visit
PUREFREEDOM.ORG

"TAKE THE PLUNGE GO DEEP!"

1

THE SPIRIT SEARCHES ALL THINGS, EVEN THE DEEP THINGS OF GOD.
1 CORINTHIANS 2:10B

WEEK 2

THE EVOLUTION!

AM I A Proverbs **7** Wild Woman or Proverbs **31** Wild Woman? } **EACH ACTION MAKES THE CHOICE.**

WEEK 3

THE **A**BSOLUTE **B**EAUTY **C**HALLENGE!

I, _____, commit to spend

_____ minutes each day all alone with the God

of the universe so He can make me more beautiful inside!

THE MARK

Aim for just one man! ········>

ONE MAN

MY VANITY FAST!

FAV VERSE!

I'm fasting from _____
for the next _____ days!

LOVE FEAST!

AT THE LOVE FEAST MY FRIENDS SAID I

[Write two inner beauty traits that your friends praised!]